A concise history of labor and work in America from the birth of the Republic to the Industrial Age and beyond

From the days of Thomas Jefferson, Americans believed that they could sustain a capitalist industrial economy without the class conflict or negative socioeconomic consequences experienced in Europe. This dream came crashing down in 1877 when the Great Strike, one of the most militant labor disputes in US history, convulsed the nation's railroads. In *The Dawning of American Labor* a leading scholar of American labor history draws upon first-hand accounts and the latest scholarship to offer a fascinating look at how Americans perceived and adapted to the shift from a largely agrarian economy to one dominated by manufacturing.

For the generations following the Great Strike, "the Labor Problem" and the idea of class relations became a critical issue facing the nation. As Professor Greenberg makes clear in this lively, highly accessible historical exploration, the 1877 strike forever cast a shadow across one of the most deeply rooted articles of national faith—the belief in American exceptionalism. What conditions produced the faith in a classless society? What went wrong? These questions lie at the heart of *The Dawning of American Labor*.

- Provides a concise, comprehensive, and completely up-to-date synthesis of the latest scholarship on the early development of industrialization in the United States
- Considers how working people reacted, both in the workplace and in their communities, as the nation's economy made its shift from an agrarian to an industrial base
- Includes a formal Bibliographical Essay—a handy tool for student research
- Works as a stand-alone text or an ideal supplement to core curricula in US History, US Labor, and 19th-Century America

Accessible introductory text for students in American history classes and beyond, *The Dawning of American Labor* is an excellent introduction to the history of labor in the United States for students and general readers of history alike.

Brian Greenberg, PhD, is the Emeritus Jules Plangere Chair in American Social History at Monmouth University, West Long Branch, New Jersey, USA. He has also taught at Lehman College, Princeton University, and the University of Delaware, where he was director of the Hagley Graduate Program from 1980 to 1987. In addition to courses on the worker in America, he has taught courses on the rise of modern America, law and society in America, and the history of American public policy.

The American History Series

Abbott, Carl *Urban America in the Modern Age: 1920 to the Present*, 2nd edn.

Aldridge, Daniel W. *Becoming American: The African American Quest for Civil Rights, 1861–1976*

Barkan, Elliott Robert *And Still They Come: Immigrants and American Society, 1920s to the 1990s*

Bartlett, Irving H. *The American Mind in The Mid-Nineteenth Century*, 2nd edn.

Beisner, Robert L. *From the Old Diplomacy to the New, 1865–1900*, 2nd edn.

Blaszczyk, Regina Lee *American Consumer Society, 1865–2005: From Hearth to HDTV*

Borden, Morton *Parties and Politics in the Early Republic, 1789–1815*

Carpenter, Roger M. *"Times Are Altered with Us": American Indians from First Contact to the New Republic*

Carter, Paul A. *The Twenties in America*, 2nd edn.

Cherny, Robert W. *American Politics in The Gilded Age, 1868–1900*

Conkin, Paul K. *The New Deal*, 3rd edn.

Doenecke, Justus D., and John E. Wilz *From Isolation to War, 1931–1941*, 4th edn.

Ferling, John *Struggle for a Continent: The Wars of Early America*

Ginzberg, Lori D. *Women in Antebellum Reform*

Greenberg, Brian *The Dawning of American Labor: The New Republic to the Industrial Age*

Griffin, C. S. *The Ferment of Reform, 1830–1860*

Hess, Gary R. *The United States at War, 1941–45*, 3rd edn.

Iverson, Peter, and Wade Davies *"We Are Still Here": American Indians since 1890*, 2nd edn.

James, D. Clayton, and Anne Sharp Wells *America and the Great War, 1914–1920*

Kraut, Alan M. *The Huddled Masses: The Immigrant in American Society, 1880–1921*, 2nd edn.

Levering, Ralph B. *The Cold War: A Post-Cold War History*, 3rd edn.

Link, Arthur S., and Richard L. McCormick *Progressivism*

Martin, James Kirby, and Mark Edward Lender *"A Respectable Army": The Military Origins of the Republic, 1763–1789*, 3rd edn.

McCraw, Thomas K. *American Business Since 1920: How It Worked*, 2nd edn.

McMillen, Sally G. *Southern Women: Black and White in the Old South*, 2nd edn.

Neu, Charles E. *America's Lost War: Vietnam, 1945–1975*

Newmyer, R. Kent *The Supreme Court under Marshall and Taney*, 2nd edn.

Niven, John *The Coming of the Civil War, 1837–1861*

O'Neill, William L. *The New Left: A History*

Pastorello, Karen *The Progressives: Activism and Reform in American Society, 1893–1917*

Perman, Michael *Emancipation and Reconstruction*, 2nd edn.

Porter, Glenn *The Rise of Big Business, 1860–1920*, 3rd edn.

Reichard, Gary W. *Politics as Usual: The Age of Truman and Eisenhower*, 2nd edn.

Reichard, Gary W. *American Politics since 1968: Deadlock and Disillusionment*

Remini, Robert V. *The Jacksonian Era*, 2nd edn.

Riess, Steven A. *Sport in Industrial America, 1850–1920*, 2nd edn.

Simpson, Brooks D. *America's Civil War*

Southern, David W. *The Progressive Era and Race: Reaction and Reform, 1900–1917*

Storch, Randi *Working Hard for the American Dream: Workers and Their Unions, World War I to the Present*

Turner, Elizabeth Hayes *Women and Gender in the New South, 1865–1945*

Ubbelohde, Carl *The American Colonies and the British Empire, 1607–1763*, 2nd edn.

Weeks, Philip *"Farewell, My Nation": The American Indian and the United States in The Nineteenth Century*, 2nd edn.

Wellock, Thomas R. *Preserving the Nation: The Conservation and Environmental Movements, 1870–2000*

Winkler, Allan M. *Home Front U.S.A.: America during World War II*, 3rd edn.

Wright, Donald R. *African Americans in the Colonial Era: From African Origins through the American Revolution*, 3rd edn.

The Dawning of American Labor: The New Republic to the Industrial Age

Brian Greenberg

WILEY Blackwell

This edition first published 2018
© 2018 John Wiley & Sons, Inc.

The right of Brian Greenberg to be identified as the author of this work has been asserted in accordance with law.

Registered Office
John Wiley & Sons, Inc., 111 River Street, Hoboken, NJ 07030, USA

Editorial Office
350 Main Street, Malden, MA 02148-5020, USA
For details of our global editorial offices, customer services, and more information about Wiley products visit us at www.wiley.com.

Wiley also publishes its books in a variety of electronic formats and by print-on-demand. Some content that appears in standard print versions of this book may not be available in other formats.

Library of Congress Cataloging-in-Publication Data

Names: Greenberg, Brian, author.
Title: The dawning of American labor : the New Republic to the Industrial Age / Brian Greenberg.
Description: 1st edition. | Hoboken, NJ : John Wiley & Sons, Inc, 2018. | Includes bibliographical references and index. |
Identifiers: LCCN 2017022272 (print) | LCCN 2017035631 (ebook) | ISBN 9781119065784 (pdf) | ISBN 9781119065555 (epub) | ISBN 9781119065685 (cloth) | ISBN 9781119065708 (pbk.)
Subjects: LCSH: Labor–United States–History. | Labor movement–United States–History. | Labor unions–United States–History.
Classification: LCC HD8070 (ebook) | LCC HD8070 .G74 2018 (print) | DDC 331.0973/0903–dc23
LC record available at https://lccn.loc.gov/2017022272

Cover Image: First Labor Day parade in the United States, New York City, September 5, 1882.
From *Frank Leslie's Illustrated Newspaper*, September 16, 1882.
Courtesy American Social History Project.

Set in 11.5/14.5pt Times by SPi Global, Pondicherry, India
Printed and bound in Malaysia by Vivar Printing Sdn Bhd

10 9 8 7 6 5 4 3 2 1

CONTENTS

LIST OF FIGURES

ACKNOWLEDGMENTS

In January 1989 I was invited by the distinguished historians John Hope Franklin and A. S. Eisenstadt to write a book on the history of labor in America in the early industrial era, 1783–1860. My book would be a volume in The American History Series, which they edited for the publisher Harlan Davidson. I was thrilled to be asked and immediately accepted, but other projects and changes in my academic and personal life continuously intervened, derailing my best intensions to finish this book. As the years passed, I would return to the manuscript for brief periods whenever I could. Fast-forward to 2014, when, during a sabbatical, I finally completed a draft of the book. I then sent the manuscript to Andrew Davidson, my editor at Harlan Davidson, which was now a part of John Wiley & Sons. Among his other responsibilities at Wiley, Andrew continued to oversee The American History Series. His response to my query about Wiley's interest in my book was to express shock as it was the first time that he had been contacted by an author who was not bowing out of a long-delayed book but was actually sending him a draft manuscript. From that point to this, once again a process that took much longer than I had planned, Andrew was all that an author could hope for in an editor. In gratitude for his abiding faith in this project and in me, I dedicate this book to him.

Andrew has since left Wiley, but my project has been ably shepherded by a number of capable individuals. In particular, I am very grateful to Janani Govindankutty for all she did to help me get my book into production and to Jacqueline Harvey for her meticulous copyediting. The draft that I sent to Andrew was reviewed by two anonymous readers, and I would like to thank them for their excellent comments. At their suggestion, I broadened the scope of the draft and, I believe, produced a stronger book as a result. I hope that they agree.

It is a pleasure to acknowledge the research support I received as Jules Plangere Chair in American Social History and from Monmouth University. These funds were immeasurably helpful in my being able to obtain the many books and articles that I used in writing this book and in giving me the time necessary to think and to write. Similarly, I am grateful for the assistance that numerous librarians and their institutions provided me in obtaining necessary sources, particularly the Hagley Library in Delaware, especially Michael Nash, and Monmouth University's Guggenheim Library, especially Susan Bucks, Linda Silverstein, Eleonora Dubicki, and George Germek. Sherri Xie in Monmouth's Interlibrary Loan office always found what I needed in an amazingly short amount of time.

A number of people facilitated the process of obtaining and reproducing the images that are included throughout the book. For their kind assistance and permission to reprint these images, I want to thank Pennee Bender and Joshua Brown, at the American Social History Project; Jane Ward, the American Textile History Museum; Bryan Wright, Colonial Sense; Robert Delap, New-York Historical Society; Jennifer Strobel, Smithsonian Institution; Lori Urso, Old Slater Mill; Arthur Gaffer, Maine Charitable Mechanical Association; Sofia Yalouris, Maine Historical Society; Peter Hansen, *Railroad History*; Steven Lubar, Brown University;

Glenn Roe, The ARTFL Project; and Shane MacDonald, American Catholic History Research Center and University Archives. I am also very grateful to Wayne Elliott at Monmouth University for all his help.

An earlier version of the history of the 1806 cordwainers' conspiracy trial appeared in *Pennsylvania Legacies* (Brian Greenberg, "Class Conflict and the Demise of the Artisan Order: The Cordwainers' 1805 Strike and 1806 Conspiracy Trial," *Pennsylvania Legacies* 14 no. 1 [Spring 2014]: 6–11). I acknowledge the journal's permission to draw from that material in this book and thank, in particular, the journal's assistant editor, Rachel Moloshok. I would also like to recognize the research support that I received from the McNeil Center for Early American Studies.

A book like this, a synthesis intended to provide an introduction for undergraduate students to the key themes and issues that confronted Americans during the dawning of labor, relies heavily on the work of others who have tilled this field. The work of my many fellow labor historians has influenced my thinking on early labor history. Although the contributions of these scholars are noted throughout the book and in the bibliographical essay, I would like to single out Irwin Yellowitz, whose course on labor history at City College of New York first introduced me to the topic of labor history, and Charles Stephenson, who was also there at the beginning of my journey as a labor historian. Finally, at Monmouth, where I have had the opportunity to work with and to learn from many excellent colleagues in the History and Anthropology Department, I especially thank the many graduate and undergraduate students who, over the years, have taken my "Worker in America" course.

Of primary importance to my being able to complete this project was the support and love I have received from my family. Kae, Molly, and now Romina are contemporary examples of the concern for others and the desire for social justice that has motivated American workers. But the writing of a book is also a practical matter. I cannot imagine having a better critic of my ideas and my writing than my wife, Susan. I have been most fortunate to be able to share with her all the highs and lows that come with writing a book.

American Exceptionalism and the Great Strike of 1877

During the presidential election of 1860, Abraham Lincoln made a campaign stop in New Haven, Connecticut. Speaking to an audience that included local shoe workers who were taking part in the "Great Strike of 1860," Lincoln asked, rhetorically, "What is the true condition of the laborer?" Using himself as an example, he responded, "When one starts poor, as most do in the race of life, free society is such that he knows he can better his condition; he knows that there is no fixed condition of labor for his whole life." Although a man "this year" might be, as Lincoln had once been, a hired laborer, he must be able to look forward to working for himself in the future and, in time, to being able "to hire men to work for him." For Lincoln, as well as for most of those in his audience, this was "the true system." Long before 1860, most Americans, or at least those living in the states that would make up the Union during the Civil War, had become convinced that the free labor system in the North represented the fulfillment of the ideals that Lincoln articulated in his New Haven speech.

The Dawning of American Labor: The New Republic to the Industrial Age,
First Edition. Brian Greenberg.
© 2018 John Wiley & Sons, Inc. Published 2018 by John Wiley & Sons, Inc.

Americans had reached a consensus about what constituted a natural distribution of wealth even before the eighteenth century drew to a close. For much of the next century, they accepted that the preservation of individual liberty required "equitability," that is, a nearly equal division of wealth among all working Americans. More an ethical standard than an economic principle, the free labor ideology bestowed property rights on all who labored. For free labor society to be practicable, each person (meaning, at the time, each adult white male) should expect to receive the fruits of his own labor. Although inequalities would persist, their assumption that today's laborer would become tomorrow's capitalist sustained free labor adherents in the belief that a natural harmony of interests existed among all classes in American society.

One of the many tragic ironies of the Civil War is that the free labor order that the Union, under Lincoln, was fighting to preserve was itself transformed by the conflict. By fostering the concentration of capital in the North, the war added to the region's already formidable forces of mechanization and undermined the social assumptions, as well as the material basis, on which the free labor ideology rested. For many of Lincoln's contemporaries, the possibility that rapid industrial expansion would produce a permanent wage-earning class created a sense of impending crisis. The poet Walt Whitman compared the "all-devouring modern word, business," to "the magician's serpent in the fable," which "ate up all the other serpents....[M]oney making is our magician's serpent, remaining today...unwieldy and immense." Even Edwin Godkin, who as editor of the new magazine *The Nation* made it the standard-bearer for free-market liberalism in the United States, recognized that "Corporations to a certain extent take the place in American society of the privileged classes of aristocratic Europe." The incompatibility of large-scale, corporate industrialism with prevailing social values would trouble Americans for the remainder of the century.

Although the progress of industrialization in the United States through the nineteenth century was uneven, within a decade of the end of the Civil War the nation was second only to Great Britain in manufacturing. Between 1860 and 1880 the total value of US manufactures more than doubled, as did the size of the industrial labor force. Expansion was especially strong in heavy industry: coal and iron production quadrupled, and the total number of steel ingots produced rose more than six times. As an example of greater economic concentration, both the number of workers and the amount of capital invested in the pig-iron industry during the 1870s nearly doubled even though the number of firms in that industry remained constant.

Yet, as understood by Whitman, Godkin, and other contemporary commentators, the critical change in the ongoing process of industrialization was less a matter of the growing size and scale of manufacturing than of the emergence of a permanent wage-earning class. In 1860 roughly the same number of workers were self-employed as were earning wages, but by 1870 wage earners and salaried employees made up the majority of productively engaged Americans, including farmers. In the industrial Northeast at this time, the odds against being self-employed – the entrepreneurial ideal of antebellum free labor society – were even greater. In Pennsylvania, for example, between 65 and 75 percent of the laboring population worked for someone else; in Massachusetts, the rate was between 75 and 85 percent. Even though the American economy remained primarily agricultural, the age of the yeoman farmer and of the economically independent producer was becoming a distant memory.

The driving of the final ceremonial golden spike in 1869 at Promontory Summit in the Utah Territory symbolized not only the completion of the transcontinental railroad but also the start of a new era of economic consolidation and expansion that further transformed America. By 1880 the railroads, the "first modern business corporation," stretched more than twice as far as they had twenty years before, linking the United States into one vast market. As business enterprises, the railroads, which required huge amounts of coal, iron, and steel, far outstripped the largest manufacturing concerns in capitalization, operating expenses, and number of employees. The Pennsylvania Railroad, the nation's largest corporation, forged an economic empire under the aggressive leadership of Thomas A. Scott that spread across the continent. Indeed, the Pennsylvania's 6,000 miles of track in the United States was outstripped by the track mileage in only two other nations, Great Britain and France.

In 1877 one of the most militant strikes in US history convulsed the nation's railroads. The private detective Allan Pinkerton compared this labor upheaval to "some sudden central volcano" that "belched forth burning rivers that coursed forth in every direction." Outbreaks of labor strife had not been uncommon in the United States before this time, but they had largely remained local brush fires. The Great Strike of 1877, however, engaged hundreds of thousands of railway and other workers and their supporters in communities across the nation in an uprising that left more than 100 workmen killed and several hundred badly wounded. Coming just one year after millions of Americans had gathered in Philadelphia at the Centennial Exposition to celebrate the country's first century of progress in industry, science, agriculture, and the arts, the 1877 strike marked the beginning of a new age of industrial conflict.

The genesis of the Great Strike lay in the depression and financial panic of the early 1870s. After the discovery in 1873 that the railroad magnate Jay Cooke had issued millions of dollars of worthless bonds, investors panicked: Wall Street crashed, banks closed, and thousands of businesses failed. Most working people, especially those in the nation's cities, found themselves either unemployed or, if not wholly out of work, then seriously underemployed. Employers repeatedly cut wages until they were only slightly more than half of what they had been just before the depression began. In no sector of the American economy was the depression's impact more severe than in the nation's rail system.

For railway workers, irregular employment and wage cuts led to a long list of grievances that accumulated especially in the wake of the panic of 1873. Work might be available for only three, four, or five days of each week, yet the men were on call for the entire time. On the days that they did have work, they labored long hours, often fifteen to eighteen at a stretch. During the 1870s depression, many rail companies stopped issuing free passes to their workers for transportation to and from their jobs, and often the cost of his trip home would be greater than the wages that the railway worker had earned that day. Even more objectionable was the policy of "doubleheaders" that was adopted in 1877 on the freight lines. Without increasing the size of the train crew, employers such as the Pennsylvania Railroad doubled the length of freight trains (going from one locomotive and seventeen cars to two locomotives and thirty-four cars per train). For rail workers "doubleheaders" meant a loss of jobs, harder work, and greater physical danger.

In March 1877, even as the railroads continued to pay their investors high dividends, the presidents of the nation's four largest lines – the Pennsylvania, the New York Central, the Erie, and the Baltimore and Ohio (B&O) – met and agreed to cut workers' wages yet again. In response, a general railway strike was called for June 24 by the newly organized Trainmen's Union, but it never materialized. Then, on July 11, John W. Garrett, president of the B&O, announced a 10 percent wage cut to take effect on Monday, July 16, for workers earning more than $1 a day. On July 16, a small group of firemen for the B&O at Martinsburg, West Virginia, refused to work at the reduced rate. The town's mayor had the men arrested, and a crowd quickly gathered, forcing their release. All the trains remained in the rail yards. Unplanned and without any central organization, the events at Martinsburg nevertheless set the pattern for strikes over the next several weeks at rail centers across the nation.

What began as a local conflict quickly spread to other industrial and transportation hubs. Within days, the uprising had shut down not only the B&O rail yards at Martinsburg but also the yards at junctions up and down the line. Moreover, inspired by the rail laborers' protest, other workers, like the canal boatmen, also walked off their jobs. After local militia companies supported the rail strikers, West Virginia officials appealed to President Rutherford B. Hayes to send in federal troops to regain control. Inevitably, armed conflict erupted between the troops and the crowds that collected to protest their presence. In Martinsburg, at least thirteen local citizens lost their lives, and fifty were wounded, during a three-day battle. After nearly two weeks, an uneasy peace finally restored service on the B&O.

Figure P.1 Labor conflict on the Baltimore and Ohio Railroad in West Virginia during the Great Strike of 1877. From *Frank Leslie's Illustrated Newspaper*, September 4, 1877. Courtesy American Social History Project.

In Pittsburgh, the strike against the Pennsylvania Railroad replicated events in Martinsburg, only on a larger scale. On July 19, the city's rail workers walked off their jobs in opposition to the Pennsylvania's effort to deploy "doubleheaders." Here again the local community was mostly supportive, and the strike soon spread to involve thousands of workers throughout the city. For the next seven days, angry crowds of strikers and sympathizers

Figure P.2   A march in Pittsburgh against the railroads during the Great Strike of 1877. From *Frank Leslie's Illustrated Newspaper*, September 4, 1877. Courtesy American Social History Project.

confronted federal troops sent to Pittsburgh to restore order, resulting in the deaths of more than fifty people and many casualties. On July 27, a fire that started among Pennsylvania's freight cars, which had been stacked up outside Union Depot, consumed 500 freight cars, 104 locomotives, and 39 buildings, resulting in a loss to the company of some $5 million. Reflecting anxieties shared by many Americans, the editor of a local paper likened the Great Strike to "the beginning of a great civil war in this country" but this time one "between capital and labor."

From Pittsburgh, the Great Strike spread to every region of the United States except New England. In the Midwest, the upheavals soon became general strikes in Chicago and St. Louis, affecting industries throughout the two cities. In St. Louis, the strike was coordinated by the Workingmen's Party, and, because local business was paralyzed, the party had effective control of the city for several days. Yet, in contrast to the pattern set in other localities, "respectable citizens" in both Chicago and St. Louis organized committees of safety to restore order. Nationwide, however, negotiations throughout the strike were hampered by the rail companies' refusal to meet with representatives of the strikers or to compromise. The railways responded to the strike, as did President Hayes, as an "insurrection" that must be "put down by *force*." After two weeks and confrontations with federal troops and armed local police forces ready to shoot directly into the crowds, the Great Strike ended.

The commercial press condemned the Great Strike as a mass rebellion, another Paris Commune of 1871, only on a much larger scale. On July 26, at the height of the disturbances, the *New York Times* characterized the strikers as:

disaffected elements, roughs, hoodlums, rioters, mob, suspicious-looking individuals, bad characters, thieves, blacklegs, looters, communists, rabble, labor-reform agitators, dangerous class of people, gangs, tramps, drunken section-men, law-breakers, threatening crowd, bummers, ruffians, loafers, bullies, vagabonds, cowardly mob, bands of worthless fellows, incendiaries, enemies of society, reckless crowd, malcontents, wretched people, loud-mouth orators, rapscallions, brigands, robber mob, riffraff, terrible fellows, felons, idiots.

Such comments reflected little of the optimism expressed by Lincoln nearly twenty years earlier that the United States could be a land of both economic progress and social justice.

The free labor ideology invoked by Lincoln had celebrated the nation's dynamic economy and the opportunity and dignity that it offered to workingmen. When acting in concert, capital and labor were thought to be part of an economic process that produced prosperity for all. Expressing these sentiments in an article on local efforts by workers to win the eight-hour workday, the *Albany (NY) Evening Journal* in the late 1860s commented, "Capital and labor are not antagonistic. They are the positive and negative elements which complete the currents and help the circuit of commerce and trade. Neither can exist without the other, and both have claims to consideration." Compare this sentiment, which echoes Lincoln's faith in the mutuality of interests, with the Reverend Henry Ward Beecher's opinions expressed in a sermon he delivered at Plymouth Church in Brooklyn on a Sunday evening during the 1877 strike. Beecher informed his congregants, "God has intended the great to be great, and the little to be little. No equalization process can ever take place until men are made equal as productive forces. It is a wild vision[,] not a practicable theory."

A month after the Great Strike ended, the treasurer of the Gatling Gun Company, which manufactured the forerunner of the modern machine gun, wrote to President Thomas A. Scott of the Pennsylvania Railroad that "the recent riotous disturbances" demonstrated the need for better preparation. Corporations like the one over which Scott presided had to "strengthen themselves *now* against such emergencies in the future by providing yourselves with Gatling guns." A few loyal employees "supplied with Gatlings afford a Railroad a perfect means of defense within itself." There is every reason to believe that Scott responded favorably to the gun company's suggestion. Not only did many corporations thereafter hire and arm private armies, but cities across the nation began construction of massive armories on land that was often donated by the local chamber of commerce.

Class lines hardened in the aftermath of the 1877 strike. Strikes during the final decades of the nineteenth century occurred with greater frequency, better organization, and more violence. During the Great Strike, the *New York Times* sadly noted that "The days are over, in which this country could rejoice in its freedom from the elements of social strife which have long abounded in the old countries." A leading historian of the era concludes that the 1877 strike threw into question one of the most deeply rooted articles of national faith – the dream of American exceptionalism. From the days of Thomas Jefferson, Americans had believed that they could have capitalist industrialism without class conflict and that the United States could avoid the negative economic and social consequences of Europe's "dark Satanic Mills." For generations of Americans after the Great Strike, "the Labor Problem," that is, the presence of fixed class relations, became the critical issue facing the country.

➤ What conditions produced America's faith in exceptionalism? What, as evidenced by the Great Strike, went wrong? We begin by looking at the world of the American worker at the time of the ratification of the US Constitution.

CHAPTER ONE

Artisans in the New Republic, 1787–1825

The Artisan Workplace

TYPO

During the early the morning hours of July 4, 1788, Philadelphia's merchants and manufacturers, among other prominent citizens, marched in a "Grand Federal Procession" to commemorate the ratification of the Constitution. With only slight exaggeration, Dr. Benjamin Rush heralded the unity of the day: "Rank for a while forgot all its claims, and Agriculture, Commerce and Manufactures, together with the learned and mechanical Professions, seemed to acknowledge by their harmony and respect for each other, that they were all necessary to each other, and all useful in a cultivated society." Sixty crafts and trades in Philadelphia took part in the celebration, marching behind carriages that depicted the city's artisan workshops. Almost every other major city in the United States held similar processions to mark the occasion. The Revolutionary War era historian Alfred Young has characterized these civic festivals as "the first 'labor' parades in American history." On this day, few appeared to question that the United States would be a society of equal and productive free men.

The Dawning of American Labor: The New Republic to the Industrial Age,
First Edition. Brian Greenberg.
© 2018 John Wiley & Sons, Inc. Published 2018 by John Wiley & Sons, Inc.

Figure 1.1   Banner of the Society of Pewterers carried during New York City's Federal Procession celebrating the ratification of the Constitution, July 23, 1788. Silk and paint; including frame, 92 × 120 × 2 3/4 in. (object #1903.12). Courtesy of New-York Historical Society.

By the time of the Constitution, artisans in the nation's port cities were fashioning a variety of consumer goods that were sold locally. An artisan or master was an individual trained in a craft such as tanning hides, barrel making (coopering), or printing. Artisans provided the skills required for the growth of cities. In Philadelphia, for example, artisans accounted for half of the city's workforce. Artisans also produced the tools used by farmers to work the land. A typical master owned his own shop, in which he worked with one or two journeymen, as well as with a number of apprentices aged between fourteen and twenty-one. But the master's role in the artisan system was based on his knowledge of the craft, not on his ownership of the means of production.

Potier d'Etain, Moules.

Figure 1.2 An eighteenth-century pewterer's shop. From Denis Diderot and Jean le Rond d'Alembert, *Encyclopédie ou dictionnaire raisonné des sciences, des arts et des métiers* (1751–72). Courtesy of ARTFL.

Figure 1.3 The interior and exterior of an eighteenth-century cordwainer's ten-footer shop. From Horace Greeley et al., *The Great Industries of the United States: Being an Historical Summary of the Origin, Growth, and Perfection of the Chief Industrial Arts of This Country* (Hartford, CT: J. B. Burr, 1872), p. 1254.

Producing custom-made goods that sold for high prices in what was called the "bespoke trade" enabled these craftsmen to secure a decent standard of living, or what was usually spoken of as a "competency" – the attainment of an independent estate of simple comforts. As Philadelphia's skilled craftsmen put it in a petition, "[T]he far greater number of us have been contented to live decently," knowing that "our professions rendered us useful and necessary members of the community, proud of that rank, we aspired no higher." Work was essential to the artisan's independence and to the general well-being of the community.

Yet, as the new century opened, expanding markets had a dramatic impact on the nature of workplace relations, especially in the nation's industrial cities and towns. For example, John Bedford, Philadelphia's largest shoemaker, facing economic ruin in 1800 as his local sales declined and his inventories built up, traveled south in search of new markets in which he could distribute large quantities of cheaply made shoes. In Charleston, South Carolina, Bedford contracted orders in excess of $4,000 for his shoes. But, once back in Philadelphia, he was confronted by irate workmen who went out on strike after he refused their demands for an increase in their wages. As a result, Bedford was forced to default on some of the orders he had secured. By 1800 small-scale manufacturing had also become common in single-industry towns like Lynn, Massachusetts. Under the handicraft system of production, master craftsmen in and around Lynn had begun producing shoes for individual customers as early as the 1760s. Known as "ten footers," Lynn's more than sixty artisan shops were usually located either in a room at the back of the master's house or in a small building attached to it.

The Political Economy of Early America

In the early years of the new republic, few leading Americans disputed the need to develop domestic manufacturing as a means of reducing US economic dependence on Great Britain.

Nevertheless, debate raged over both the sites and the scale of the manufactures and over whose economic interests would prevail. For Tench Coxe, an enthusiastic promoter of early American industrial growth who served as assistant to the secretary of the treasury, Alexander Hamilton, the endless potential of America's vast natural resources would remain forever untapped without manufacturing. Under Hamilton's guiding hand, Coxe's "Plan for a Manufacturing Society" led, in 1791, to the creation of the Society for Establishing Useful Manufactures (SUM), a government-promoted attempt to harness private capital on behalf of developing a "National Manufactory," a model industrial town to be built in New Jersey.

Hamilton's and Coxe's ambitious plans to encourage manufacturing aroused intense opposition. One influential opponent, George Logan, a prominent Philadelphia Quaker physician and agrarian democrat, led the forces arrayed against the National Manufactory. In 1792, in the pages of the *American Museum*, Coxe and Logan squared off in a debate over the SUM. Logan attacked the National Manufactory as a "dangerous scheme" that threatened the nation's republican order. Fearful of any activity that would encourage citizen dependence on government or worker dependence on another individual for economic well-being, Logan supported decentralized, small-scale manufacturing, either in urban craft shops or in households scattered across the countryside. Logan and other critics of the SUM endorsed a small-producer tradition that encompassed a faith in the social utility of skilled labor, an expectation of moderate prosperity or competence for workers, and an intense commitment to equality and community.

Both Coxe and Logan understood that each member of society should also be a stakeholder in it. Both men regarded independence as the key, although they defined the concept differently. For Coxe, independence meant providing the United States with a balanced and interdependent economy that included manufacturing. He believed that the social and moral dangers inherent in industrialism, especially the formation of a dependent wage-earning class, could be avoided through both the employment of immigrants, poor women, and children and the introduction of power-driven, labor-saving machinery. For Logan, only an agrarian-based economy that included small-scale household manufactures would preserve the dream of American exceptionalism.

Coxe was, of course, sensitive to agrarian objections to the growth of manufactures. He insisted that the introduction of manufacturing would not upset the natural balance of employment. The objection that manufacturing takes male farm laborers from agriculture was not "solid," he declared, since "women, children, horses, water and fire" perform four-fifths of the labor in manufactories. As he repeatedly asserted, "our people must not be diverted from their farms." More to the point, Coxe expressed an almost unlimited faith in the *labor*-saving capability of mechanization. The concern expressed about manufacturing being unhealthy was, he observed, "urged principally against carding, spinning and weaving, which *formerly* were entirely manual and sedentary occupations." Instead, it is "our plan" that machines using "*the potent elements of fire and water*" become "*our daily labourers.*" In 1813, expanding on their labor-saving capabilities, Coxe wrote that "these wonderful machines, working as if they were animated beings ... may be justly considered as equivalent to an immense body of manufacturing recruits, enlisted in the service of the country." Coxe anticipated that continued improvements in the "construction and application of machines" would mitigate the high cost of labor in America.

The labor force that Coxe foresaw working in the factories – women and children, the poor, and immigrants – would also mitigate another "principal objection" to manufacturing in America, the alleged scarcity of skilled labor in the United States. The model, according to Coxe, was England, where, with waterpower and machines, "a few hundred women and children" performed the work of twelve hundred carders and spinners. "Justice, policy, and benevolence ought to excite us" to adopt a similar system in the United States. "Every city man is taught a trade or calling; every country man is taught the same or to plough, harrow, sow, and thresh. Every city and country woman should be taught to card, spin, weave, and dye." A few years before the founding of the SUM, Coxe had encouraged the Pennsylvania Society for the Encouragement of Manufactures and Useful Arts (PSEMUA) to open a mechanized spinning mill in Philadelphia that would provide employment for the poor while, coincidentally, demonstrating "the importance of cotton manufactures to this country ... as a source both of private and public wealth." The labor force working in the PSEMUA's textile mill was mostly female, and the mill's network of spinners in the city and surrounding countryside was entirely so.

Yet, in contrast to Coxe's rosy view, many Americans of the founding fathers' generation expected the consequences of further manufacturing growth in the United States to reproduce the same malignant social and moral conditions, as symbolized by Manchester's "dark Satanic Mills," that they saw afflicting England. Thomas Jefferson declared that the present "manufactures of the great cities in the old country" produced "a depravity of morals, a dependence and corruption, which renders them an undesirable accession to a country whose morals are sound." Large-scale manufacturing would produce an army of dependent workers that would be corrosive of republican virtue. Referring to manufacturing, Jefferson observed, "Dependence begets subservience and venality, suffocates the germ of virtue, and prepares fit tools for the designs of ambition." Jefferson's own best hope for America rested instead on promoting a self-reliant and independent citizenry through husbandry.

In this respect sounding very much like Jefferson, Coxe too worried about the corrosive influence of dependence, but he saw a solution in the expansion of employment through manufacturing. Coxe told those gathered to launch the PSEMUA that "extreme poverty and idleness in the citizens of a free government will ever produce vicious habits and disobedience to the laws, and must render the people fit instruments for the dangerous purposes of ambitious men. In this light the employment of our poor in manufactures, who cannot find other honest means of a subsistence, is of the utmost consequence." Coxe counted the inculcation of proper habits in the poor as a primary benefit of manufacturing. An "idler" was "ever prone to wickedness," whereas "habits of industry" filled the mind "with honest thoughts" by "requiring the time for better purposes." Industriousness leaves little leisure "for meditating or executing mischief." "All is the gift of industry," Coxe wrote. "Among individuals it is the supreme virtue; and, when well ordered and duly regulated, it is the only criterion of a good and wise government." In *The Mills of Manayunk: Industrialization and Social Conflict in the Philadelphia Region, 1787–1837*, Cynthia Shelton notes that, in employing the labor of the poor, the PSEMUA mill, much like other early textile manufactures in Philadelphia, was modeled on English and colonial workhouses. In this way, the PSEMUA functioned like a public agency, encouraging the development of industrious habits and self-discipline.

Coxe's appointment in May 1790 as assistant secretary of the treasury was due in part to Alexander Hamilton's desire to have on his staff someone with the ability to defend him in print against his detractors and in part to Hamilton's willingness to respond to political pressure put on him by Coxe's allies. Having been enjoined by Congress in January 1790 to produce a report on manufacturing, Hamilton turned over to Coxe responsibility for collecting the necessary data. Although Hamilton would eventually come to regret this appointment, his collaboration with Coxe reached a high point in 1791, the year that the Hamilton *Report on Manufactures* was issued and the SUM was founded.

[Called "the most ambitious industrial experiment in early American history," the SUM received a charter on November 22, 1791, from the New Jersey legislature.]Overall direction of the society was entrusted to its board of directors, and the supervision of its operations to a governor, William Duer, a wealthy New York speculator. Besides being granted the usual powers of a manufacturing corporation, the SUM was given banking privileges, generous tax exemptions, and the corporate powers of a city. Within a month, shares in the society to the value of $625,000 had been subscribed (although not fully paid in).[In May 1792, after three society meetings and some wrangling, a site on the Great Falls of Passaic was chosen and named Paterson, in honor of the then governor of New Jersey.]

Although the society had been chartered to make any commodity it wanted, at the May meeting the SUM's manufacturing committee adopted a resolution "to erect a cotton-mill, also buildings for carrying on calico-printing, with requisite machinery, together with buildings to accommodate workmen." Appropriations were made of $20,000 for the construction of a canal, $5,000 for the cotton factory and machinery, $12,000 for the print works, and $5,000 for the weave shop and equipment. The committee agreed, as well, on plans to complete the town, including a plan to construct fifty dwellings, on quarter-acre lots, for employees. Organizers anticipated little trouble finding an available workforce from among unemployed people, or rather, according to Peter Colt, second superintendent of the SUM, those "people who are not fully employed – and an abundance of women and children, who are without regular useful employment."

The society proudly announced in June 1794 its completion of "a large mill for spinning cotton by water-power." The celebrations in Paterson for the opening of the mill included a great parade and a ball given in the factory. Despite the high hopes aroused by these early efforts, the society was already in financial trouble. The SUM was never able to secure adequate capital, at least in part because of a financial panic that, in the spring of 1792, landed Duer in debtors' prison. Nor were the problems only financial ones. The National Manufactory also suffered from poor management, labor shortages, and, at times, insufficient power from the Great Falls. In January 1796 the society's directors adopted a resolution suspending mill operations.

The ambitious plans to build a National Manufactory in Paterson intensified the deep suspicions that had already been aroused by Hamilton's economic program. Among the most outspoken critics was the Quaker physician George Logan, a committed physiocrat (follower of the eighteenth-century French economists who asserted that land was the true source of all wealth), who after Jefferson's presidential victory in 1800 would be elected to office and, ironically, become one of Coxe's closest political allies in Pennsylvania. In a series of "Five letters addressed to the yeomanry of the United States," published in the *American Museum*, Logan issued a philippic against the "dangerous scheme" of Hamilton, Coxe, and the other leaders of the SUM. These letters summarize the fears Logan shared with others who were opposed to the founding with government support of a manufacturing town in New Jersey.

In the opinion of "A Farmer," as Logan pseudonymously signed himself, the SUM was an agency of special privilege and corruption, antithetical to the "general interests" of the community. Like Jefferson, Logan assumed that the Paterson site had been chosen mainly because of its proximity to New York and the city's "junto of monied men," a suspicion confirmed in the critic's mind by Hamilton's support for Duer's election as SUM governor. Often taking Adam Smith's *Wealth of Nations* as his text, Logan insisted that "we ought not to desire the establishment of any kind of manufacture in our country, which cannot support itself, without government granting to its agents bounties, premiums, and a variety of exclusive privileges." The equation was simple for Logan: when the few gained special privileges, the general interests suffered.

Citing examples from the ancient world as well as the more contemporary experiences of France and England, Logan condemned government interference and protection in what should be private matters. Less a laissez-faire censure of government action, Logan's critique expressed greater concern that "all partial regulations" tended to create "separate interests in society." Logan feared that economic differences in the distribution of property would harden into a fixed class order. Could it be doubted, he asked rhetorically, that "the nature" of the SUM was such that the society subverted the "spirit of all just laws" and thereby established "a class of citizens with distinct interests from their fellow citizens? Will it not by fostering an inequality of fortune, prove the destruction of the equality of rights, and tend strongly to aristocracy?" The result, Logan had no doubt, would be the division of society into "two-parties," one enjoying "the comforts of life, without labour – the other languishing in penury."

The greatest danger, in Logan's view, was that the SUM would transport the social structure of the manufacturing towns of England to the American countryside. Likely with the SUM's projected workforce in mind, he decried "the combination of the wealthy" in the English towns who kept the poor "employed by them in a state of daily dependence and servitude." To symbolize what should be the natural relations in a just society, Logan employed the analogy of a chain, which "does not derive its strength and utility from being composed of a few heavy links, and the remainder weak." Every link must be, as much as possible, of equal power. The combination of power under government patronage that was being accumulated in Paterson appeared to Logan to be no less than a conspiracy against the social compact.

Government that is run on behalf of the privileged few erodes the opportunity that each individual should have to freely express his talents. "The wealth of private citizens at their own free command, and employed by themselves," he insisted, "will ever be the greatest advantage to their country." And in civil society,

Logan asserted, "a state is rendered more respectable and powerful by the prosperity of all its citizens." Rather than doom the many to "mere animal existence," each member of society was owed the promise of achieving a moderate well-being or competency. For democracy to prevail required that every manufactory provide an equivalent to labor that would enable a worker to live in simple comfort, to educate his children, and to provide for the support of his family after his passing. Competency promised a degree of comfortable independence.

Many of the other republican opponents of the SUM sounded themes similar to the ideas Logan presented in his five letters. "Anti-Monopolist" bemoaned "the present propensity for corporations and exclusive privileges, a system of politics well calculated to aggrandize and increase the influence of the few at the expense of the many." Another critic blasted the "Jersey Manufacturing Company," calling it "an institution ... opposed to the principles of a republican government." According to "A Mechanic," in supporting the SUM Congress was "granting to some exclusive privileges, premiums, and exemptions from the common burthen." Building large manufactories at government expense was "*in effect, planting a Birmingham and Manchester, amongst us.*" As did Logan, these protagonists considered the [SUM to be a dangerous assault by a privileged few against the common weal.]

By invoking the dangers inherent in the English textile centers of Manchester and Birmingham, critics of the SUM, in common with Logan, expressed widely held fears that a concentration of wealth and power represented a threat to the political as well as to the economic system of the United States. Such concerns, however, did not make either Logan or the other agrarians blindly anti-manufacturing. Jefferson loved experimenting with labor-saving gadgets; as one biographer says of Monticello in the years after Jefferson returned home, "Here was no pastoral Eden but belching smoke and clanging hammers." In 1800 Logan helped found the Lancaster County Society for Promoting of Agriculture, Manufactures, and the Useful Arts. In the preamble to its constitution, which he is credited with writing, Logan makes the surprising observation that "Independent Communities do not owe their characters to the Soil which they occupy; but to their Progress in the useful Arts." Yet, as he makes clear, the Lancaster County Society had no "desire to make this, in the common acceptation of the Word, a Manufacturing Country." Even less did the society desire to introduce into this "happy Country, that baneful system of European Management which dooms the human Faculties to be smothered, and Man to be converted into a Machine. We want not that unfeeling plan of Manufacturing Policy, which has debilitated the Bodies, and debased the Minds, of so large a Class of People as the Manufacturers of Europe." Logan, like Jefferson, assumed that large-scale enterprise would produce an army of dependent workers, "a degeneracy ... a canker which soon eats to the heart" of a republic's laws and constitution, in the words of the Virginian. In place of the intensive mill community planned by the SUM, Logan proposed extensive, decentralized household production as the basis for developing "virtuous" manufactures in the United States.

Along with Logan's letters, the *American Museum* printed a response from Coxe, who was identified as "A Freeman." Coxe rejected the notion that the SUM was a "dangerous scheme." In his view, rather than serving special interests, government encouragement of manufacturing furthered the general welfare. "Measures intended for the public good, and really calculated to produce that desirable end," Coxe wrote, "have been [either] honestly misunderstood, or wilfully misrepresented." Yet Coxe's views on the appropriate realm of government action did differ fundamentally from the ideas expressed by Logan. For Logan the lessons of history taught that there could be no interference by government in "the occupations of citizens" that would not result in "injury." America and Americans would be independent only to the degree that they had "the liberty to manage their own affairs." Coxe, in contrast, believed that national self-sufficiency required an active state that vigorously promoted economic growth.

Coxe regarded a diversified economy that included manufacturing as an antidote to dependence. The demand for raw materials required by manufacturing, Coxe had written, would enable "the planter and the farmer to vary their articles of produce exceedingly, which will prevent that reduction of prices which must follow the cultivation of a small number of articles." So too would economic diversity benefit the farmers of the Middle States. Without manufactures, Coxe insisted, "the progress of agriculture would be arrested" on Pennsylvania's frontier. Similarly, without an expanding rural population, manufactures would languish. A broadly based and interdependent national economy, Coxe had concluded, would be a source of independence for the individual and for the nation both.

Despite their serious differences, Coxe and Logan are not simply the opposite poles on some late eighteenth-century political or economic scale. In fact, Coxe had himself, in the 1780s, excoriated the directors of the Bank of North America for creating an exclusive monopoly, "not only a monopoly, but an aristocracy, formed of a most formidable kind, a monopoly which, by acquisition of the function of government, will be capable of absorbing all the wealth of the United States. And as wealth creates influence, it is impossible to tell how far their influence may extend." During the 1790s, Coxe expressed similar misgivings about Hamilton's economic program. In *Liberty and Property: Political Economy and Policy Making in the New Nation*, John R. Nelson, Jr., catalogues numerous differences between Coxe's proposals and Hamilton's fiscal program. For example, whereas Hamilton's *Report on Manufactures* mentioned funding the SUM solely through government bounties as a means of stabilizing the financial market, the draft prospectus that Coxe had prepared for the treasury secretary concentrated on stabilizing credit to stimulate investment in manufactures. In fact, as Cathy Matson and Peter Onuf, in *A Union of Interests: Political and Economic Thought in Revolutionary America*, have noted, Coxe became suspicious of the people that Hamilton had recruited for the SUM. He worried about "the close ties between this 'monied interest' and British merchants and creditors." Unlike Hamilton, whose economic program aimed mainly to bind (and benefit) the interests of a wealthy elite to the new government, Coxe believed in popular participation in politics and in the need to sustain economic opportunity. By the end of the decade, Coxe had joined the Republican Party, having formally broken with Hamilton and the Federalist Party in 1794 over Jay's Treaty, an agreement with Great Britain that did not contain any English concessions on impressment or the rights of American shipping.

The Early Transformation of the Workplace

Shortly after George Washington visited Lynn during a tour of New England in 1789, the demand for shoes increased beyond the boundaries of the local market. To meet the needs of the growing market, shoe manufacturers introduced the domestic, or "putting-out," system. Lynn merchant-manufacturers like Ebenezer Breed sought to simplify and speed production. They worked through local agents, contracting with skilled journeymen to cut the shoe leather and then distributing the leather pieces to "shoe binders," women who lived in the farm households surrounding Lynn and who stitched together the upper parts of shoes. Female shoe binders adapted their traditional needle skills rather than learn the entire trade as apprentices. During these years, wives and daughters were recruited to the task of shoe binding as unpaid labor by the male head of the household. Like their domestic duties, shoe binding became another way in which women contributed to the family economy.

After 1810 the female shoe binder, although still working in her home, was hired and supervised by a merchant-manufacturer and performed a job that was paid for in wages or in store goods. The partially made shoes would then be finished (or "bottomed" – the fastening together of the sole, heel, and upper parts of the shoe) by the skilled journeymen before Breed and his fellow shoe merchants in Lynn could ship the final product to Philadelphia, New York, and other seaport cities for sale in "slop shops" or to the South and the West Indies, where they were purchased for slaves to wear.

Beginning in the 1820s, however, local shoe bosses collected the skilled journeymen who cut the leather and bottomed the shoes into central shops, generally two-story wooden buildings located in Lynn, in which all the steps (other than binding) in producing shoes and selling them could take place. Micajah C. Pratt, the son of a shoe manufacturer, was born in Lynn in 1788 and entered the shoe business in 1812. The following year, he built a small shop that would serve as his manufactory until 1850. By 1832, Pratt was employing some 200 men and women to produce "cheap, strong, and durable shoe[s]" that he distributed to customers in the South and West. Pratt, Breed, and other local entrepreneurs had by then raised the annual output of shoes in Lynn to nearly a million pairs.

In the leading port cities of Philadelphia and New York and in the countryside around them, as well as in one-industry towns like Lynn, markets expanded as the eighteenth century drew to a close, giving rise to a concentration of production in consumer goods trades such as shoemaking and clothing manufacture. As a result, the work process was divided and transformed. As the number of goods produced increased, master craftsmen were displaced by merchant-manufacturers who did not themselves make anything but instead purchased and distributed the raw materials, owned the workplace and supervised those working there, and collected and sold the final product. Under these conditions, artisans could no longer confidently look forward to owning their own shops. More and more, they faced a work life bound by wage labor. By 1820 some 12 percent of the US labor force worked for wages, and by 1860 the proportion reached roughly 40 percent, with most of these wage earners residing in the North.

Yet even as the manufacturing entrepreneurs attempted to obtain the greatest output of goods at the cheapest cost, journeymen fought back, looking to uphold the traditions of the "Trade" and to secure a "just price" for their labor. As early as the mid-1790s, both manufacturers and journeymen began to organize separate associations to promote their increasingly competing interests. Merchant-manufacturers founded general societies as semipolitical umbrella organizations to help them oversee the trades and to secure favorable legislation, especially higher protective tariffs, from the national and local governments. They also relied on these societies in their efforts to reshape mechanics' morality and work habits to fit the demands of the more competitive workshops.

Although workplace relations were still largely harmonious, the reorganization of production in the 1790s resulted in journeymen organizing among themselves. In Philadelphia, for example, the city's shoemakers, viewing themselves as victims of the new workshop order, first briefly in 1792 and then more permanently in 1794, founded the Federal Society of Journeymen Cordwainers. By the end of the second decade of the nineteenth century, printers, carpenters, cordwainers (shoemakers), tailors, cabinet and chair makers, and other journeymen in the seaport cities had organized collectively and formed labor unions. Thus, long before the mechanized factory became the typical workplace in America, standardization of product, specialization of labor, and contested relations between employer and employed already characterized what became known as the "American system of manufactures."

Rural Manufactures

Despite a doubling of the population over the last third of the eighteenth century to reach a total of some five million, the United States in 1800 remained overwhelmingly rural. Roughly

80 percent of Americans worked on farms, and many others depended on the products of the farm economy for their living. By contrast, only one in ten Americans worked primarily in manufacturing. In 1820, according to the census, fewer than one in ten Americans lived in urban places (communities with 2,500 or more people). Of these urban residents, more than half could be found in just six seaport cities: New York, Philadelphia, Boston, Baltimore, New Orleans, and Charleston. Almost nine-tenths of American agriculture and manufactures was concentrated along a strip only 100 miles inland from the Atlantic.

In the early republic, Americans produced for themselves most of the basic necessities that they required. The family remained the primary economic unit. Roughly two-thirds of the clothing that farm families wore between 1810 and 1820 was homemade. From December to May of each year, many farm households concentrated on indoor activities such as spinning and weaving. Spinning, the twisting of short woolen fibers into continuous threads on a simple spindle, was women's work. Weaving could be done on looms by either men or women. Some looms were small enough to be placed on a person's lap, and some were so large that they filled an entire room. Writing in her diary in the 1790s, a teenage Elizabeth Fuller records having spun and then woven some 176 yards of cloth. When she finished on June 1, she rejoiced, "Welcome sweet Liberty." But her sense of freedom must have been fleeting. Although the cloth Elizabeth produced most likely filled her family's needs for that year, the sewing of the shirts, petticoats, and breeches that they wore still had to be done.

The pattern of rural life does not quite conform to the Jeffersonian image of the independent, self-sufficient yeo*man* as the backbone of America. First, the output of wives and daughters who labored alongside husbands and sons was essential to the farm family's material prosperity. Even though particular activities would be distinguished as "men's tasks" and "women's tasks,"

Figure 1.4   An example of a family employed to produce cloth in their home during the "putting-out" period in the early textile industry. From Edward Hazen, *The Panorama of Professions and Trades; or Every Man's Book* (1836). Courtesy of American Textile History Museum, Lowell, MA.

the work of the rural household required the mutual cooperation of every member of the family. Second, like the farm family, farm communities were of necessity mutually interdependent. Farm families frequently assisted one another, sharing tools and lending a hand when a task such as harvesting or barn raising required extra help. In her diary, Martha Ballard notes that she and her daughters produced cloth, raised garden produce, preserved vegetables, and did the household chores even while she performed the duties of a midwife for local families.

Although rural folk are justifiably famous for their versatility, no farm family could alone accomplish all the tasks – the sewing, knitting, baking, gardening, brewing, dairying, candle making, stone masonry, butchery, wood chopping, blacksmithing, leatherworking, carpentry, reaping, plowing, and so on – that sustained any farm. Only plantations or the wealthiest farmsteads could afford to have their own gristmills or sawmills. They would either hire the services of a miller or have these tasks performed by slaves or indentured servants. Much more often, gristmills and sawmills in the early nineteenth century were operated as neighborhood industries in which millers turned the farmers' wheat into flour and sawyers turned trees into lumber for local use. The mill operators might receive cash in return, but frequently their payment was in the form of produce, homemade goods, or labor. Other small neighborhood industries – ironworks, paper mills, wool carding and fulling mills, tanneries, brickyards, and the like – were also common in the early nineteenth century, particularly in older, more settled communities.

One prototypical mill town was Rochester, New York. Before the completion of the Erie Canal in 1825, four- and five-story stone flour mills dominated the city's center and its economy. Boats would pull up alongside the mills, located near waterfalls on the Genesee River, and workmen would shovel the grain from the vessels into buckets on the water-powered vertical conveyors that carried the grain to a mill's top floor. Based on plans developed by the American inventor Oliver Evans in the 1790s, machinery then cleaned the grain and ground it into flour, which was packed into barrels for distribution. Paid in cash for their wheat, the Genesee Valley farmers bought the guns and nails, shoes, hats, wagons, farm tools, and other manufactured necessities, as well as the luxuries like jewelry and mirrors, that were produced by local skilled artisans who made up more than half of the adult men in Rochester.

The rural artisan, required to be a jack-of-all-trades to earn his living, usually practiced more than one craft. One enterprising Long Island artisan "advertised himself as a clockmaker, carpenter, cabinetmaker, toolmaker, and a repairer of spinning and weaving equipment as well as guns – all while collecting fees for the pasturing of other people's cows." Especially in the more populous East, but to a certain extent in small frontier communities as well, a considerable number of craftsmen traveled from farmhouse to farmhouse to ply their trades. These cobblers, blacksmiths, curriers, coopers, hatters, tailors, weavers, and shoemakers lived with the family and utilized the raw materials of the farm. Most rural areas included a few itinerant artisans, such as carpenters and blacksmiths, who often worked at their trades only part-time. Weavers and shoemakers traveled from house to house doing custom work, or "whipping the cat," as it was known. William Bolton, a farmer living in Northampton, Massachusetts, hired two local women to come to his house to spin and weave cloth for his family. Not surprisingly, he ceased hiring women outside his family in 1803 when his daughter became old enough to do some of this work herself.

In 1791 the US treasury secretary, Alexander Hamilton, observed that the countryside was a "vast scene of household manufacturing," where rural folk produced clothing, shoes, and other necessities, "in many instances, to an extent not only sufficient for the supply of the families in which they are made, but for sale, and even in some cases, for exportation." Twenty years later, his counterpart in the James Madison administration, Albert Gallatin, found that the average farmer's house in New Hampshire had at least one spinning wheel and that every second house contained a loom on which 100 to 600 yards of saleable cloth could be woven annually. The household production of goods made primarily for family use peaked around 1815. A marked decline in household production took place thereafter, first in the East and then, between 1830 and 1860, in most parts of the country.

Born in Andover, Massachusetts, in 1786, Caleb Jackson, Jr., grew up on a fifty-acre farm in nearby Rowley. Because Caleb decided at the age of fifteen to keep a journal, a record exists, brought to light by the historian Daniel Vickers, of how and why an otherwise unexceptional farm family came to participate in household production in early nineteenth-century America. Even though the family farm was well located near the active commercial centers of Salem and Newburyport, Massachusetts, the Jackson acres barely provided enough to keep family members employed. Seeking to preserve its independence, the Jackson family began to make apple cider not only for their own use but also for those neighbors who brought their apples to be pressed in the Jackson cider mill. The Jacksons also hired out the labor of male members of the household as shoemakers. Beginning in 1803, during the winter months Caleb, Sr., bought cut leather from the local agents of wealthy merchants in Newburyport and Lynn for his sons to stitch and make into shoes. Never commanding the dignity of independent farming, shoemaking appears to have been viewed by Caleb as an "unpleasant obligation," something "we have got to [do]" in order to achieve a satisfactory way of life. The Jacksons put a high premium on comfort and improvements to property. Caleb's diary notes that the family used the proceeds from their outwork production to build a new end to their barn and a bigger cider mill, as well as to remodel the shop and construct a new house with six fireplaces, nine rooms, and twenty-seven windows. In his diary, Caleb never refers to individual advance but rather to that of "we," meaning his collective family. Outwork became for the rural Jackson family, as it had been for many of their urban artisan contemporaries, a means by which they could achieve a comfortable independence.

In an excellent overview of the transformation of women's work in the Industrial Revolution, the historian Thomas Dublin observes that during the early decades of the nineteenth century "the handweaving of machine-spun cotton yarn into cloth and the braiding of split palm leaf into men's and children's hats" became important industries for farm women in New England. As their farm chores diminished during the winter and early spring months, unmarried teenage daughters took to weaving yarn from the local spinning mills or braiding palm leaf hats for the local storekeeper to sell. Middlemen supplied or "put out" the necessary materials, collected the completed work, and attempted, with minimal success, to impose some measure of discipline over their labor force.

Using the surviving account records in the 1820s of one such middleman, Silas Jillson of Richmond, New Hampshire, Dublin looked to learn more about the place of outwork in the lives of rural residents. Widespread in Richmond, outwork weaving appears to have provided rural families with a modest supplement to their agricultural production. The output of a typical weaver was only four yards per day. Even in the winter and spring months, weaving probably took up only three days of a weaver's week. Both male and female household members were account holders with Jillson, but the records do not indicate who did the actual weaving. Nevertheless, Dublin concludes that the data suggest that a family's unmarried daughters did most of the outwork weaving, under either their own account or that of their parents. Unmarried daughters made up almost two-thirds of women with accounts, and their earnings from weaving were comparable to those of the male household heads.

In the rural countryside, the clothing trades were not simply extensions of women's household labor. Women and men worked together to support their families. According to the historian Marla R. Miller, rural clothing production is best understood as "an artisanal craft ... in which both men and women participated vigorously, though in different ways that responded very differently to changing circumstances." For example, in tailoring, a distinction has to be made between the cutting and the sewing of a garment and whether the article of clothing was being made for a male or a female client. Miller cites as one example of these distinctions the purchase by Frederick Wardner in the fall of 1800 of two and a quarter yards of coating from the shop of the Windsor, Vermont, merchant Isaac Green. Wardner brought the material to a tailor who measured him and cut the pieces for a new overcoat. He then took these pieces to a Windsor "tailoress," Catherine Deane, who made the garment. Thus a sort of division of labor, or what Miller refers to as "hierarchies of skill and status," existed "that turned on the gender of both a garment's maker and its user." A "tailoress" was likely a woman who sewed but did not possess specialized skills in cutting, whereas a "tailor" could be either a man or a woman who possessed the skill to both cut and sew men's apparel.

Outwork families tended to be larger than other rural families and to have more teenage children (especially daughters, whose work shifted back and forth from agricultural tasks to weaving). Also, because weaving required the expense of either building or purchasing a loom, as well as enough space in a house to use it, outwork families were usually somewhat better off than their poorer neighbors. With the rise of the power loom in the 1820s, handloom weaving, which at its peak employed 12,000 outworkers across rural New England, declined precipitously. By 1829, the year that Jillson closed his accounts, outwork weavers were experiencing severe cuts in the prices paid per yard for their output. However, a new form of outwork, the braiding of children's and men's palm leaf hats, was expanding, becoming by 1837 an industry valued at $1.9 million and employing more than 51,000 women and children across rural New England.

The growth of palm leaf hat making in the 1820s and 1830s resulted more from the spread of the industry over a larger area than it did from mechanization or a more intense work process. Storekeepers distributed to local farm families the palm leaf used in making the hats, which they bought wholesale from Boston merchants who imported it from the West Indies. Looking at account books of a Fitzwilliam, New Hampshire, store owner and middleman, Dexter Whittemore, Dublin found that, like handloom

Figure 1.5 "Scenes and Occupations Characteristic of New England Life." From *Ballou's Pictorial Drawing-Room Companion*, June 16, 1855. Courtesy of B. Davis Schwartz Memorial Library, Post Campus of Long Island University.

weaving, hat making was a major source of income for farm families in the area. Outwork was taken up by farm families less because of desperate need than because it provided a supplementary source of income that fitted well with the rhythms and demands of the other activities of a farm household. Like the handloom weaver families, palm hat maker families tended to be larger than their neighbors, usually due to differences in the number of daughters. However, the families that made palm hats were often poorer than handloom textile families. As one Vermont braider in the 1830s explained, "Money is so scarce and we must have some." Even though younger girls, married women, and widows also braided palm leaf hats, most palm leaf hat makers were teenagers.

In the main, outwork supplemented the income of the fathers' farms. In 1830 Whittemore employed more than 250 individuals who in that year produced 23,000 hats. Increasingly, his outworkers lived on farms located farther and farther from his store. Farm families braided hats, a seasonal activity, for about 78 full days a year. Even though they earned on average only $20.68 in credits at Whittemore's store, for some outworkers, such as widows, hat making became a steady, if modest, source of income. The income from palm leaf hat making was often used by the children of farmers to help them prepare for their futures. Dublin found that farm daughters spent about two-thirds of their store credits on sewing supplies, while their brothers used their credits to purchase household furnishings and agricultural implements. Thus the farmers' daughters appear to be purchasing the goods they needed to make clothing and linen for their future households, and the sons the goods they would need on the farms that they expected to establish.

During the first half of the nineteenth century, outwork had a significant impact in rural communities in the Northeast. Farm families were able to supplement their income from agriculture and to sustain themselves in the face of greater competition from more productive farms in the Midwest. Outwork provided an alternative to factory employment for farm women. Working at home and entirely unsupervised, they could help maintain the family's income. Yet, because of the central role played by the store owner and the middleman, outworkers were not self-employed producers. They experienced an early form of wage labor, earning not cash but store credits. From the start, merchants installed small workshops in which the finishing process for the palm leaf hats was carried out. These shops were enlarged during the 1840s and 1850s, and women were hired to work in them. Finally, by the 1850s, production was consolidated in factories and only braiding was left in the hands of male and female outworkers. Rural outwork is best understood, Dublin concludes, as a transitional phase of industrial labor, one that merged earlier labor practices with new ones.

By the 1820s, local traders and urban merchants such as Bedford, Breed, and Pratt had already begun to create a dynamic intraregional market in farm produce and household-manufactured goods. Their entrepreneurship enabled towns like Lynn to take full advantage of the emergent interregional trade that resulted from a revolution in the nation's system of transportation. By the end of the second decade of the nineteenth century, improvements in roads, bridges, turnpikes, and inland canals, often financed at least in part by the national and state governments, had created an infrastructure that made commerce and travel infinitely easier. These improved means for moving goods and people resulted in enlarged markets and helped foster an industrial revolution in the United States.

The Economy of Seaport Cities

Prior to 1820, the seaport cities of Boston, New York, Philadelphia, Baltimore, New Orleans, and Charleston had become depots for transoceanic shipping. Even though in the early 1800s most manufacturing took place in the countryside, the concentration of population in these six centers of maritime commerce created an expanding market for locally made as well as imported goods. Carpenters, coopers, rope makers, caulkers, sailmakers, bricklayers, distillers, printers, tanners, and other artisans produced the commodities that met the everyday needs of the city dwellers for goods and services as well as provided the more expensive clothing, household furnishings, and other luxury items desired by well-to-do urban merchants and professionals.

Seaport cities also required the services of many unskilled casual or day laborers to load and unload ships, cart merchandise to and from the docks, and perform a great many heavy manual jobs. The laborers, stevedores, seamstresses, and other casual workers constituted about 40 percent of the urban working class. They were paid about $1 or less per day in 1800, and the evidence from Philadelphia and other seaport cities indicates that their wages improved little over the next three decades. Their living standards were deplorable. In the 1790s, according to one New York physician, many families among the laboring poor lived in "decayed wooden huts" surrounded by muddy alleys and permeated by the stench of "putrefying excrement." These workers, usually employed only irregularly, were a highly transient group whose circumstances made organized resistance highly unlikely.

An artisan system of production flourished in Philadelphia and the other American seaport cities at the turn of the century. No single trade dominated Philadelphia's manufactures. Even the shipyards, perhaps the city's largest employer, would have hired no more than two dozen men each. The pace of work in artisan production was at best casual. The master and his journeymen and apprentices worked by hand to fill orders or to build up a small inventory of goods for sale from the shop. As independent producers, the city's mechanics owned their tools and lived either in the workshop or within walking distance of it. Performing their jobs in ways that would have been familiar to their fathers, the city's masters and journeymen derived great pleasure from their work. The master, as Karl Marx observed, owed his role in production more to his knowledge of the craft than to his ownership of the means of production. Each mechanic who began as an apprentice assumed that he would one day be a master himself. The transition of the young apprentice to journeyman and then master appeared to be part of the natural cycle of a workingman's life.

Although each apprentice and journeyman could reasonably expect to have an "equal chance for his share of business in his neighborhood," the goal of these mechanics was a competency rather than great wealth. A competency was more than simply an economic reward. The craft shop was structured like a family, and the intimate ties of the masters, journeymen, and apprentices encouraged the subordination of self-interest in favor of a commitment to the collective well-being. Well into the nineteenth century, competency remained the expectation of every working person and underlay an implicit understanding between workers and their communities.

Drawing on the traditions of the American Revolution, artisans commemorated their contributions as the producers of society's wealth. The membership certificate of the New York Mechanics Society in 1791 depicted at its center the muscular arm of a workman holding a hammer above which is written the society's motto, "By Hammer & Hand all Arts do stand." The certificate included images of a turner and his assistant working on a piece of furniture at a lathe, a blacksmith at his forge, and a farmer plowing his land. Another image celebrated the members' mutual obligation to care for one another by showing a representative of the society bringing aid to the widow and children of a deceased member. As mechanics, they took pride in the contribution that their labor made to the general well-being of society.

At Fourth of July and other annual celebrations, mechanics assembled and marched in procession through the streets of their communities, proclaiming their allegiance to the principles of artisan republicanism. Reflecting this attitude, an orator speaking to a group of artisans in New York at an Independence Day celebration in 1810 extolled the virtues of "republican simplicity" and the "genius of America," which were predicated on "just notions of Liberty" and "founded upon the RIGHTS OF MAN." The mechanics took pride in their crafts and celebrated the political, social, and economic independence to which they were entitled as productive citizens. Wary of unrestrained competition and unlimited accumulation, artisans advocated a republican order based on equal rights, the social value of labor, competency, and their understanding of community as an association of individuals who labored for the benefit of all.

Manual Labor In and Out of the City

Prior to the beginning of construction of the Erie Canal in 1817, only 100 miles of canals had been completed in the United States. The phenomenal success of the Erie stimulated a canal-building boom that resulted in the construction of some 3,326 miles of canals by 1840. Yet, the panic of 1837 and the economic depression that followed, as well as the tremendous expansion of railroad building, would bring the canal era to a close by the end of the 1850s. In terms of its management structure, technology, and system of labor, canal building in the United States was, from the first, a mix of the old and the new.

Speculative commercial enterprises, canal-building projects were organized as joint-stock companies chartered by the state. Canals were expensive endeavors, and they had to be fully built before tolls could be collected and they could become profitable businesses. Those at the top of the canal management structure – the proprietors, the president and board of directors, engineers, and overseers – increasingly relied on contractors or independent builders to construct these artificial waterways. The canal companies mobilized an unusually large labor force. Unlike other contemporary workplaces such as the small artisan shops, the emerging urban manufactories, and outwork, the larger canals required from 500 to 1,000 workers. Even in the early years, by one estimate more than 3,000 men were engaged in canal construction.

The hard and often dangerous work these "canallers" performed did not change much throughout the history of canal building in the United States. Most canal jobs were simple and familiar; the work was accomplished mainly by pick, shovel, auger, wheelbarrow, and cart and was powered by gunpowder, oxen, horses, and humans. Only a few jobs, such as constructing the locks, which involved stonecutting and masonry, required workers who were more skilled. Although the wages paid to canal workers were comparatively high, the irregularity of the work resulted in low overall earnings. Canal workers, who were mostly casual laborers, that is, hired by the job and constantly on the

Figure 1.6 Workers on the Erie Canal in the early 1830s. Aquatint. From the John Hill Print Collection (image #46562). Courtesy of New-York Historical Society.

move, were paid only for the number of days they worked, and interruptions due to weather, injury, illness, or company financial problems were common. Even those who found more regular work averaged only seventeen and a half days per month. Working from dawn to dusk, usually twelve to fourteen hours in the summer and around ten in the winter, canal workers were expected to be punctual and diligent or they would see their pay docked.

In the early phase of canal development, prior to 1816, canal companies utilized all forms of labor. Canal workers included slaves (mainly in the South), who were either hired or purchased; indentured servants, who were bought directly off the ships in the harbors along the Atlantic coast; and free workers (mainly in the North), who were contracted by the year, month, or day. In 1826 a visitor to the Chesapeake & Delaware Canal found some "2500 men constantly at work, Irish, Dutch, Welsh, French, Swiss, and Negroes." As a result, the canal workforce was diverse – African American slaves; English, Dutch, and Germen free workers who were already living in the United States; and newly arrived Irish immigrants.

Canal laborers lived in "Corktowns" or "Slabtowns," family shanties or all-male barracks located near the worksite or in a nearby town. Stigmatized because of their racial and ethnic backgrounds as well as their rough work and living conditions, canal laborers, until the 1830s, tended more to fight among themselves over issues such as the limited number of jobs available than to join together in opposition to their employers. As a visitor to the Chesapeake & Ohio Canal noted, "The Irish and Negroes kept separate from each other, for fear of serious consequences." More often, conflict arose from the canallers' resentment of their marginal existence than from any sense of solidarity with their fellow workers.

Not surprisingly, the life of a slave laborer on the canals was different from that of a free worker. Slaves were usually hired for the year or half-year but sometimes for shorter periods, especially as management's desire for a more flexible labor force developed. The fee was paid to the master, and it depended not only on the labor supply but also on the dangers that the work posed for such a valuable property as a slave. Nevertheless, about half the cost to the canal companies of employing slaves, like that for free laborers, derived from the need to supply food, shelter, and clothing for these workers. Such costs, of course, were not a factor in the casual labor market in the nation's cities.

In 1800 Baltimore surpassed Boston to become the third largest city in the nation. The Maryland city's shipyards, small workshops, and early manufactories attracted a skilled workforce that supplied Baltimore's residents with furniture, shoes, barrels, jewelry, and many other goods as well as built the ships that sustained the city's commercial progress. Yet many of Baltimore's workers labored outside the craft workshops, in the streets as casual labor. "Scrapers" removed the manure, and stevedores and carters loaded and unloaded ships. Casual laborers also carted grain into Baltimore from the Maryland and Pennsylvania countrysides or worked as millhands who ground the wheat that arrived into flour. White women stitched shirts by candlelight in their apartments or "hawked" candles, cheeses, and vegetables in Baltimore's neighborhoods. Many African American women labored as laundresses. Both free and enslaved African American men and women worked as domestic servants in the city's public accommodations and wealthier households. As the historian Seth Rockman has noted, "Whether male or female, native born or immigrant, Euro-American or African American, enslaved or free, these working people struggled to scrape by."

To dredge the Inner Harbor, Baltimore, for thirty years beginning in 1790, funded the operation of a "mudmachine." The Irish immigrant Michael Gorman, arriving in Baltimore in 1793 having fled from his master in Philadelphia, became a mudmachine worker twenty years later. Like Gorman, hundreds of mudmachinists maneuvered scoops of muck, emptied them into waiting scows, and delivered the dirt as landfill for waterfront properties. Although the mudmachinists earned slightly higher wages (a little more than $1.10 a day) and worked more steadily than the city's other common laborers, they still lived a marginal economic existence. Typical of unskilled laborers in Baltimore and elsewhere, they owned no tools and the casual nature of their work denied them job security. Unlike Gorman, few mudmachinists were able to establish their own households. For mudmachinists, unlike the city's artisan workforce, the "grueling and filthy" work that they performed was not a stage in a life that would eventually lead them to economic independence, but an occupation that offered them little or no chance of advancement.

Engaged mainly in unpaid – what is often referred to as "invisible" – labor that ensured the well-being of the family and the household, women had few occupational choices in Baltimore or elsewhere in the United States in the early nineteenth century. Yet, as the port city's economy expanded, jobs that had been performed at home by mothers and daughters, such as washing, feeding, and sheltering, were becoming part of the city's service economy, that is, work done for pay. Free African American women worked as laundresses. Slaves and indentured servants worked in Baltimore's taverns and inns. Free black, immigrant, and native-born women were employed as domestics, supplying household help for the city's middle-class families. Although now paid, few such forms of labor available to women in Baltimore could provide them with a reliable subsistence.

However, as Rockman has observed, "[T]he commercialization of women's traditional household labor" did have "one key group of beneficiaries: free African American laundresses who could now support themselves on the labor that had previously been coerced within slavery." In 1817 Baltimore, 77 percent of the city's laundresses were African American women. Free women were able to do the washing at home, independent of direct supervision by their employers. For the African American women who came to dominate the laundry business, such work represented an opportunity for a better life.

In 1816 four women hucksters protested a fine of several dollars levied against each of them for violating a new city ordinance that prohibited selling outside the confines of Baltimore's covered marketplaces. "Poor, necessitous, and indigent," and having "no mechanical trade, no manufacturing faculty, no stock," the women could obtain no other employment "whereby they cou'd obtain a scanty subsistence for themselves and [their] families." Mostly poor, white, and widowed, female hucksters would, a decade later, oppose a new state licensing law that they insisted would deny them their "humble but lawful Traffic." In a plaintive appeal to the community's self-interest, they claimed that "by this oppressive law" they will be compelled "in all probability ... [to] be thrown upon the charity of your city and [be] forced to become the unfortunate Tenants of your Alms House." Despite their pleas, the selling of goods on the streets proved untenable.

Commonly referred to by historians as unskilled, the laborers who dug the canals through the countryside or dredged the harbors or sold goods on the streets of America's cities did the necessary work that advanced the economy of early America. A much more diverse group than those who labored in the nation's artisan shops, casual workers would come to protest their working conditions only later, in the 1830s. Unlike the craftmen of the late eighteenth and early nineteenth centuries, whose protests were triggered by changes in the nature of skill and the control of production, unskilled workers were largely demonstrating against their declining material conditions.

Economic Change and the Demise of the Artisan Order

In the late eighteenth century, masters and journeymen began forming joint self-help associations such as the General Society of Mechanics and Tradesmen (1785) in New York City, the

Association of Mechanics and Manufactures (1789) in Providence, Rhode Island, and the Franklin Typographical Society (1793) in Philadelphia. These mutual benefit societies were mainly concerned with helping unemployed members and with providing health, widows', and burial benefits. Yet, despite the harmony of the artisan workshop attested to by these societies and celebrated in the many Grand Federal Processions of 1788, the bonds formed in the craft shop were starting to fray by the century's close.

Beginning in the 1790s, economic change transformed the artisan system of production in the workshops of the nation's seaport cities. For example, in Philadelphia, instead of fashioning a pair of custom-made shoes for every shop patron, Bedford and other up-and-coming merchant entrepreneurs began to produce shoes in greater volume, offering them ready-made for sale in local retail markets or in new markets in the West Indies and in southern cities such as Charleston, Savannah, and New Orleans. To increase output and reduce the cost of labor, the merchant entrepreneurs reorganized their shops: instead of having a journeyman make the whole shoe himself, the work was divided into discrete tasks, each performed by a different worker. Shoe manufacture in Philadelphia took on the essential features of a market society in which a worker's labor was viewed as a commodity – valued in terms of cash and subject to the supposedly impersonal laws of the free market.

The rise of the merchant entrepreneur undermined the mutualistic social relations that had been customary in the craft shops. In place of the mutual benefit societies they had organized with their masters, journeymen began in the late 1780s to form nascent trade unions. Most of the new unions were local and brought together journeymen from a single craft. The unions charged their members a small initiation fee and set dues at six to ten cents per month. As journeymen lost faith in the old dream of becoming masters and accepted the likelihood that they would remain journeymen for their entire working lives, they saw unions as agencies for self-defense against their increasingly organized employers.

In 1786 twenty-six journeymen printers in Philadelphia organized a union, the Typographical Society, to protest a reduction in their wages. The society called the city's first labor strike, which was settled on the workers' terms. But the interests of the employing masters and their wage-earning journeymen continued to diverge. As their working conditions deteriorated, journeymen articulated their sense of the chasm opening between themselves and their masters. By 1817 the New York Society of Printers had come to understand that "the interest of journeymen [is] separate and in some respects opposite to that of employers." Some two dozen strikes in New York between 1795 and 1825 reflected the growing unity among urban workers as the gap between them and their employers widened.

Taking a practical approach to the changing structure of work, these early labor organizations developed practices that would later be associated with the term "business unionism." As the labor historian Melvyn Dubofsky has pointed out, the first unions looked "to protect members against the dilution of craft standards, increase their income, shorten hours, and improve working conditions through agreements with their employers." They enforced strict rules that compelled members to abide by wage and work standards. Seeking job security for workers at a time of growing insecurity, they also demanded that members and employers accept what was the equivalent of a "closed shop," that is, a shop in which only union members could be hired or retained. Those workers who refused to join the union or to abide by its rules were condemned as "scabs," reviled by one Philadelphia cordwainer as "a shelter for lice."

One major issue that the skilled journeymen confronted was that of "run-away" apprentices, or competition from the growing number of not fully trained workers that employers hired to cut costs. The traditional apprentice being initiated into "the art and mysteries" of the trade was usually a boy (but could also be a girl), aged fifteen to sixteen or even younger and often the son (or daughter) of a relative or close friend of the master. Throughout the colonial period, apprentices helped meet what would otherwise have been a labor shortage. Records show that 1,075 youths were apprenticed in Philadelphia over the two years between October 1771 and October 1773. Formal apprenticeship required a contract between the youth's parents and the master that set out the articles of indenture. The new unions sought to enforce strict rules limiting the number of apprentices to be employed in a shop. Thus the Philadelphia Typographical Society, which excluded from membership anyone "who shall not have served an apprenticeship satisfactory" to the union, demanded that all printing positions in the city be reserved for its members.

Facing an assault on traditional practices from their employers, journeymen attempted to establish what they considered to be fair working conditions. The workday in most urban workshops paralleled that on the farm, from sunup to sundown throughout the year. In 1791, in the first recorded "turnout," or strike, in the building trades, the Journeymen Carpenters of the City and Liberties of Philadelphia sought, in addition to increased wages, overtime pay and a reduction in their work hours. The journeymen complained that they had "heretofore been obliged to toil through the course of the longest summer's day" and declared that in the future "a day's work amongst us shall be deemed to commence at 6:00 in the morning and terminate at 6 in the evening of each day." Although the masters scoffed at the journeymen's claim that "*self-preservation ... has induced us to enter into indissoluble union with each other*" and rejected the workers' attempt to set their conditions of labor, the "contagion" that the employers feared led to more strikes.

The strike by the Philadelphia Journeymen Carpenters in 1791 was conducted in much the same way as many of the early turnouts. Unions did not negotiate across a table with their employers as they do today; instead, they drew up a list of demands, which a delegation presented to the employer or which the union publicly posted, and then waited to see if their employers accepted or rejected their conditions. Rather than specifying an "increase in wages," journeymen in these years usually called for a "just price" for their labor. What precipitated the conflict is unknown, but in 1794 a journeymen's association, the Federal Society of Chair Makers in Philadelphia, submitted its own book of prices to the clerk of the district of Pennsylvania. When, the following year, the association again tried to set the price for its members' labor, the city's masters replied that they "would not employ any journeymen cabinet-makers as society men, but [only] as individuals." Nevertheless, evidence suggests that in 1796 both parties agreed to a price book that included a cost-of-living clause for the workers that allowed the "prices" they were paid to respond to increases in the cost of the "necessaries of life, house-rents, &c."

Just as they did when they tried to set the hours of their workday, journeymen distinguished between the boss's assertion of his right as owner of the business to set wage levels and their right as producers to set the price on the value of their labor. For the journeyman the price of his labor should be determined by what he needed to maintain a respectable household rather than on what the product would sell for in the market. As one journeyman tailor claimed in 1819, "[T]he Journeyman is better able to decide upon the merit of his labor than the employer is for him." Viewing themselves as the producers of all wealth, the journeymen rebelled against the notion that their labor was a commodity to be purchased by employers at the lowest possible price.

Cordwainers, or shoemakers, were among the most militant journeymen at the turn of the century. In 1794, in Baltimore, the United Journeymen Cordwainers went out on strike against the master shoemakers over alleged abuses of the apprentice system.

The masters, the journeymen complained, failed to properly train the eight to ten apprentices who served in each shop. The United Journeymen demanded that in the future only two apprentices be instructed and that the journeymen rather than the masters take charge of their training. The employers refused to change the apprentice system. In another example of the journeymen shoemakers' propensity to engage in "collective bargaining by fiat," in 1799 at least 100 cordwainers in Philadelphia walked out following the master shoemakers' flat rejection of wage demands presented to them by a workers' deputation. In this instance, however, both sides appear to have ultimately agreed to "split the difference."

Six years later, journeymen cordwainers in Philadelphia again demanded wage increases and were again immediately turned down by their masters. A bitter strike ensued that lasted six to seven weeks. According to the strikers, the shoe merchant entrepreneurs were no longer producers; instead, they had become "mere retailers" of the cordwainers' labor, living in luxury off the workers' output. The strike proved disastrous for the journeymen. Not only were they forced to return to work at the old rates but some forty members quit the society. Of greater consequence, the masters, embittered by more than fifteen years of constant labor strife, decided to challenge the journeymen's association in the courts. In November 1805 eight members of the Journeymen Boot & Shoemakers of Philadelphia were arrested and charged with forming an illegal "combination and conspiracy" to raise their wages and with restraint of trade. The indictment claimed that the defendants had attempted to exact "great sums of money" from their employers by refusing to work "at the usual prices and rates," by forming themselves into "a club" and making "unlawful and arbitrary by-laws," and by using threats and other unlawful means to prevent their fellow craftsmen from working. Their trial, *Commonwealth v. Pullis* (1806), was the first of a dozen conspiracy cases that over the next two decades would undermine not only the cordwainers' union but also the entire early labor movement.

The conspiracy trial began in Philadelphia in March 1806. Prominent lawyer-politicians from Philadelphia's contending political parties represented the two sides in the dispute. Jared Ingersoll and Joseph Hopkinson, both ardent Federalists, served for the prosecution, while Walter Franklin and Caesar Rodney, staunch Jeffersonians, argued for the defense. Hopkinson's opening remarks made clear to the jury that the journeymen "are not indicted for regulating their own individual wages, but for undertaking by combination to regulate the price of labour of others as well as their own." This he branded coercion. The first witness, the shoe worker Job Harrison, testified that a journeyman's failure to join the workingmen's association and to abide by its rules would lead to his being "scabb'd": the other workers "would not work in the same shop, nor board or lodge in the same house, nor would they work at all for the same employer." Hopkinson condemned such rules as acts of a "secret society" that were clearly "injurious to the general welfare."

The prosecution quickly pointed out where it believed the community's general interest lay. Hopkinson appealed to the jury – which included two innkeepers, a merchant, two grocers, a tobacconist, a watchmaker, and a master tailor – to remember that Philadelphia "is a large, encreasing, manufacturing city." A vast quantity of manufactured goods was exported to the West Indies and the southern states. "It is then proper," he called on the jury, "to support this manufacture. Will you permit men to destroy it, who have no permanent stake in the city?" In the view of the prosecution, right-thinking members of the community – those with a stake in its continued well-being – needed to come together to end this threat to the city's economic prosperity and to punish the conspirators. Hopkinson even suggested that in acting to hold down wages the city's merchant-manufacturers were serving the good of the community because they were thereby keeping the price of goods low. For the prosecution, only the needs of the employer, as the property owner, and not those of the laborer who actually produced the material objects, were worthy of consideration.

The defense, of course, had a different view of where the community's welfare rested. By seeking to determine the rate "at which the journeymen should work" without consulting "the wishes of the workmen," the "*would-be masters* had united against them," according to defense counsel Franklin. The journeymen had freely united to resist "this state of slavish subordination." In a public address during the strike, the journeymen had pointed out that they had assembled for the last fifteen years "in a peaceable manner for our common good." By such acts as assisting "those that age may [have] rendered incapable of labor," the cordwainers' association helped "to promote the happiness of the individuals of which our little community is composed." No person, the defense claimed, had been compelled to join the society. Rather, the journeymen had joined together as free agents on behalf of their collective self-interest.

Rodney challenged Hopkinson's characterization of the journeymen cordwainers as mere "birds of passage" who had no stake in society. He called on the members of the community represented by the jury to recognize that labor, too, had social value. It was labor, he insisted, that constituted "the real wealth of the country." All that the journeymen had done by submitting a list of wages that they believed they should be paid was commit "the unpardonable sin of setting and ascertaining the price of their own worth." To "establish the principle, that laborers or journeymen, in every trade, are to submit to the prices which their employers, in the plentitude of their power choose to give them" would be "to destroy the free agency of this meritorious part of the community."

Rodney's point about who should set the price of labor was made even more bluntly in Philadelphia's *Aurora* by the newspaper's radical democratic editor, William Duane, who charged the employers with attempting to reduce the city's laboring men to a "breed of *white slaves*" forced to live in "a condition still more despicable and abject." The best method for advancing Philadelphia's manufactures, Rodney assured the jurors, would be "to secure to workmen the inestimable privilege of fixing the price of their labour." It was as producers that they voiced their collective best interests, and it was on this assumption that the defendants rested their claim to consideration by the community.

The conspiracy trial ended in 1806 in a defeat for the eight journeymen shoe workers. On the morning of March 28, the clerk read the jury's verdict: "We find the defendants guilty of a combination to raise their wages." The actual punishment meted out by the jury – the Philadelphia cordwainers were fined $8 each and the costs of the suit – was relatively mild. Nevertheless, the guilty verdict meant that, although the workers could join together to provide benefits for each other, they could not legally attempt either to set the price of their labor or to determine who would be able to work in a specific trade.

Having failed to free themselves from dependence on their "so-called masters," the journeymen looked to produce shoes on their own. A month after the trial ended, the Journeymen Cordwainers announced that they had opened a warehouse where they intended to carry on a boot and shoe business, both wholesale and retail. The shoe workers had determined, they told the public, that they could either go into business for themselves or submit to employers "who could take away or lessen their wages whenever their caprice or avarice might prompt them." Despite the cordwainers' high hopes for their cooperative, as far as is known the venture was not a success.

Workers' efforts to gain control over their labor persisted long after the end of the cordwainers' strike of 1805 and the conspiracy trial that followed. Beginning with the formation of the first unions and continuing throughout the nineteenth century, a culture of opposition arose that sought to rally the "producing classes" against what they would, starting in the 1820s, condemn as "wage slavery," or the fear that wage labor was becoming a permanent and deteriorating condition in the United States. Like the cordwainers, most workers in America understood that each individual craftsman had property rights in the goods produced by the labor of his hands. A moral vision of a producers' republic encompassed an alternative understanding of labor and property under capitalism, one that went beyond an expectation of decency and fair play in the relations of production to envision a system of capital ownership in the United States in which there was "no hire at all."

Celebrating the New Era

On November 4, 1825, New Yorkers throughout the state held a day of carnival, parade, and general jubilation to mark the official opening of the completed Erie Canal. The New York City celebration was the climax of ten days of noisy festivities known as the Wedding of the Waters because Governor DeWitt Clinton deposited in the Atlantic Ocean bottles of water that he had filled earlier from Lake Erie.

Towns along the canal route had boomed with the start of construction in 1817. When the canal reached Rochester in 1821, the village's population, which a decade earlier had been "without a house or an inhabitant," had reached 1,500. In 1825 Buffalo, which had been a sleepy village of some "thirty to forty houses" in 1810, was a community of some 2,660 inhabitants. The canal would be completed in four sections, and at the peak of its construction the 363-mile-long waterway required the services of some 4,000 canal workers.

Much as the Grand Federal Procession marking the ratification of the Constitution had done nearly forty years earlier, the canal celebrations in New York City and elsewhere brought together all members of the community. In New York City the colorful parade wended its way from Greenwich Street through the streets of Lower Manhattan to end at City Hall. Grouped by occupation and affiliation, leading clergymen, members of the local medical society, Freemasons, and city officials marched behind representatives of Clinton's alma mater, Columbia University, and associations of coopers, bakers, tailors, potters, sailors, and teachers. Most of the craft associations carried large banners, and some rode on elaborate wagons that demonstrated the operations of their trades.

The journeymen, marching together with their masters in craftsmen associations but also separately as members of their newly formed societies, honored the long traditions and ancient symbols of their crafts and celebrated the canal's completion as a modern example of American technological achievement, progress, and prosperity. Held aloft, the grand standard of the Chair-Makers' Society, an artisanal association, depicted a female figure with a cornucopia, a common symbol of peace and plenty. Her left hand rested on an ornate chair, and in the background was a chair manufactory. The society's motto proclaimed, "By Industry We Thrive." On the reverse of the standard was the chair makers' coat of arms, adorned with two chairs and a carpenter's tool on the crest. The master craftsmen marched behind the grand standard and were followed by eight boys who held aloft a large gilt eagle grasping a miniature chair in its beak. Members of the Journeymen Chair Makers Society came next, another eagle, and finally the apprentices, who held a banner emblazoned with the words "Peace and Liberty."

Like the chair makers, the city's other trades paid tribute to the worthiness of industry and to their trades' contribution to the peace and prosperity of the community. Journeymen tailors carried a banner that depicted a "Native" receiving a cloak over which was their motto, "Naked Was I and Ye Clothed Me."

Carrying the same banner that they had in 1788, the coopers erected a platform on which two men and a boy (a symbolic master, journeyman, and apprentice) built a large cask. And on their float, the printers worked presses that turned out odes in honor of the day. Many of the banners and insignias contained patriotic symbols and republican images.

In addresses delivered throughout the day, masters and political leaders, as they had during the earlier Grand Procession, extolled the virtues of united effort. Celebrating the harmony of the occasion, they observed that such achievements were made possible by "the common bond and mutual sympathy," and the "ties and attachments ... interwoven with the strongest feelings of the heart," that they believed governed the building of the canal. The celebrants invoked the Erie Canal as a symbol of what would later become known as the free labor system, an affirmation of the nation's dynamic economy and of the opportunity and dignity presumably offered to all members of the community. In the official outdoor celebrations throughout the day, homage was paid to the unity of all members of the community. Nevertheless, the commercial and middle-class New Yorkers who attended elite gatherings in the evening chose to honor only the work of the canal's commissioners, as well as the foresight of the politicians and of the citizens who had elected them. As Carol Sheriff, a leading historian of the Erie Canal, notes, the evening's speakers celebrated how such "virtuous citizens would protect the common good." Sheriff also points out the noticeable absence of the canal's common labor force from the day's festivities, "They did not sing public odes, march in parades, or offer toasts." In their idealization of the mutuality of the artisan system, the celebrants ignored the friction then disturbing harmonious relations in their workshops. A growing discontent had led the journeymen to express their sense of solidarity with each other by marching together in their own, separate associations. Yet, even as they affirmed their independence through these associations, many of the journeymen also believed that they came together not out of self-interest but on behalf of the common good. In the decades that followed the opening of the Erie Canal, workers expressed through their unions and strikes their hopes that the promise of a more equitable and cooperative industrial order for all Americans would be fulfilled.

CHAPTER TWO

Labor in the Age of Jackson, 1825–1843

The Geography of Industrialization

The official opening of the Erie Canal in 1825 represented a turning point in the transportation and market revolutions that redrew the economic map of the United States in the first half of the nineteenth century. Before 1820 the nation's natural barriers had placed severe limitations on internal commerce. As a result, moving a ton of goods some thirty miles inland cost about the same as shipping the same goods 3,000 miles across the Atlantic Ocean. But, beginning around 1815, with the invention and commercial development of the steamboat, the canal boom that followed the completion of the Erie Canal, the building and upgrading of roads and turnpikes, and the early development of a national railroad network, the cost of moving goods within the continental United States plummeted. A trip between New York City and Cincinnati, Ohio, that took almost two months in 1817 could be completed in a week by the early 1850s. Because people and goods could now be moved more

The Dawning of American Labor: The New Republic to the Industrial Age,
First Edition. Brian Greenberg.
© 2018 John Wiley & Sons, Inc. Published 2018 by John Wiley & Sons, Inc.

easily and cheaply, the nation's urban population grew, and new areas of the West opened up to settlement. Reliable access to new markets encouraged American manufacturers to produce a greater diversity of commodities in ever-increasing quantities. By 1860 Americans who labored on farms and in manufactories and factories were producing goods and services worth between $2 billion and $3 billion.

The transportation revolution not only stimulated a market revolution; it also transformed the workplaces of those who labored in both the rural countryside and the seaport cities of the New England and Middle Atlantic states. As we have already seen for such early industries as boot making and shoemaking, the demands of intensified output led to a division of labor and a simplified work process that undermined skill. After the Erie Canal was built, manufacturing continued to grow as a component of the American economy. Yet the progress of industrialization through the first half of the nineteenth century was uneven. Especially in cities, handicraft industry and outwork persisted even as large mills and giant factories materialized on the rural landscape.

The impact of the Erie Canal on life in the local communities along its route can be illustrated by what happened in Rochester after 1821, the year that the canal reached this busy village in western New York. In *A Shopkeeper's Millennium: Society and Revivals in Rochester, New York, 1815–1837*, Paul Johnson, a leading historian of early economic change, called Rochester, until then a small village that processed wheat grown by farmers in the surrounding Genesee Valley, America's first inland boomtown. Within a few years of the canal's opening, Rochester's population of some 1,500 mushroomed by almost 700 percent. In 1834 Rochester was rechartered as a city. Provided by the new canal with access to the New York City market, farmers expanded their holdings and vastly increased the amount of grain they produced. The number of flour mills in Rochester grew, as did the

Typo re-chartered

number of manufactories that produced for sale in the city and surrounding countryside such necessary goods and small luxuries as guns, iron nails, shoes, hats, woolen cloth, wagons, furniture, farm tools, and even jewelry and mirrors. In 1827 only 21 percent of the adult males in Rochester were still independent proprietors. The other four-fifths worked either as journeyman craftsmen or as laborers doing casual work on the canal, in the mills, or in construction helping to build the growing village. The organization of work also changed. The shoemaker, cooper, and other craft workers not only experienced a dilution of their traditional skills but were also subject to greater discipline in the workplace.

Prior to 1850, New York City was the leading manufacturing center in the United States. The historian Sean Wilentz, in *Chants Democratic: New York City and the Rise of the American Working Class, 1788–1850*, describes manufacturing during these years in cities like Newark, New Jersey, New York, and Philadelphia as "metropolitan industrialization." Although factories using steam-powered machines had begun to appear, industrialization in these cities was still dominated by machineless factories and outwork manufactories that were the backbone of what Wilentz characterizes as "the bastard artisan system." These factories tended to employ at least twenty workers. Now more closely supervised, factory workers carried out traditional handicrafts in an intensive and subdivided routine. Before 1812, ready-made clothing was unusual in America. Garments were made either in artisan shops by tailors and seamstresses or at home by wives and daughters. By 1850, in New York and other urban centers, outwork manufactories had become the largest employers. In them, a small number of men worked on the garments that required more skill and fitting, completing their tasks in the shops. The outworkers, women who performed the lesser-skilled operations, labored in cellars and garrets throughout the city. Even after 1820, the manufactories that came to dominate the garment trade could not completely supplant smaller and family-owned businesses in the urban areas. Specialization, including traditional custom work, persisted. Nevertheless, during the 1820s and 1830s, four out of five masters in New York lost control of their shops and rejoined the ranks of the journeymen. By the 1840s, the prospect of becoming self-employed was increasingly unlikely for most journeymen.

The Erie Canal's phenomenal success alarmed business leaders in the nation's other commercial centers. In Pennsylvania, a "building craze" ensued that led the state to develop its own canal system. The market revolution that came after the construction of the state's canal system contributed to a growth in manufactures in Philadelphia, just as the Erie Canal had done for New York City. By 1860 the Quaker City's industrial output would be second only to New York's. In *Working People of Philadelphia, 1800–1850*, the historian Bruce Laurie describes industry in Philadelphia at midcentury as a diverse mix that included artisan or neighborhood shops in which handwork persisted; nonmechanized factories with more than twenty-five workers; sweatshops in the footwear and apparel and other consumer goods industries; outwork manufacturies that relied on the putting-out system, such as in tailoring, shoemaking, weaving, and a few other marginal industries; and factories powered by steam or water. About 15 percent of the city's workforce was made up of unskilled day laborers who worked as needed, mostly in commerce and construction. In Philadelphia, as in New York in the two decades following completion of the Erie Canal, the work was now harder, the workplace was larger, and the workers were more closely supervised. Overall, the workers seem to have lived better in 1820 than they did in 1850.

Much the same can be said for workers in other manufacturing centers in the United States. Even before 1820, centralization of production was well under way in the shoe industry in Lynn, Massachusetts. As the market expanded, merchant-manufacturers followed the example set by Micajah Pratt in 1813 and opened central shops that employed journeymen shoemakers in greater numbers than they had been in the craft workshops. Women continued to work at home as shoe binders, and their employment spread throughout the New England countryside. In fact, by the 1830s in Massachusetts, there were more women binding shoes than there were working as operatives in cotton textile mills. Now paid directly by the piece by Lynn's central shop owners, the rural female outworkers could be more independent of the family wage system. Nevertheless, married women still had to combine shoe binding with their household tasks. By the early 1830s, Pratt and other merchant entrepreneurs like Isaiah and Nathan Breed and Isaac Newhall employed more than 200 men and women, and the separation between owners and workers – capital and labor – became more pronounced.

Like journeymen elsewhere, Lynn shoemakers fared poorly as a result of the changes in production. Intense competition drove down the price of shoes and, in the era before the sewing machine, persuaded shoe manufacturers to increase productivity by hiring more "hands" and increasing the hours of work. In 1810 the Lynn shoe industry had turned out a million pairs of shoes valued at $800,000; by 1836 Lynn produced two and a half times the number of pairs and their value had more than doubled. By 1830 and possibly even earlier, Lynn's journeymen shoemakers had become full-time wage earners whose well-being was determined solely by the payment they received to produce shoes. The prospect of their becoming self-employed masters faded into memory.

The introduction of labor-intensive techniques into handicraft manufacturing in industries like shoemaking was one path to industrialization that was followed in the United States. Beginning with small firms in the 1790s, textile production demonstrated a second path that was based on capital-intensive production in large factories containing extensive power-driven machinery. In 1790 Samuel Slater arrived in Pawtucket, Rhode Island, to assist Moses Brown, a wealthy Quaker businessman, and his son-in-law, William Almy, in building an English-style textile mill. Slater, a recent migrant from England, had learned the British textile industry as an apprentice to Jedidiah Strutt, a prominent Derbyshire cotton manufacturer and a partner of the Richard Arkwright who had pioneered British textile manufacturing. After experimenting for a few years, Slater, Brown, and Almy opened Old Pawtucket Mill, a two-and-a-half-story "factory house" in which nine workers, seven boys and two girls, used water-powered machinery to card, or clean raw cotton and separate it into threads, and to spin, or twist the threads on spindles to turn the threads into yarn.

Figure 2.1   Samuel Slater. From J. D. Van Slyck, *New England Manufactures and Manufacturories: Three Hundred and Fifty of the Leading Manufacturers of New England* (1879). Courtesy of American Textile History Museum, Lowell, MA.

Figure 2.2   A drawing of the original 1793 Slater Mill. Courtesy of the Old Slater Mill Association.

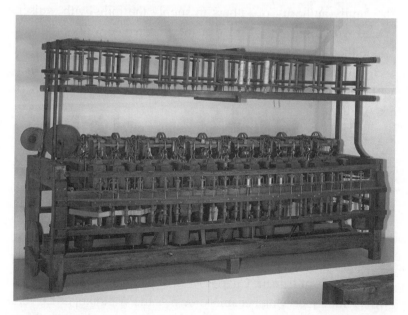

Figure 2.3   Slater's spinning frame. Courtesy of Smithsonian Institution, National Museum of American History, Home and Community Life.

Highly successful, Slater and his associates constructed more, even larger textile mills, and by 1807 the partners controlled approximately one-fifth of the cotton-spinning industry in the United States. In what historians call the family, or Rhode Island, system, early Slater-type mills were built, at a cost of between $10,000 and $30,000 each, on rural sites next to sources of water-power. Looking to recruit entire families, Slater-type companies constructed mill villages that provided employees with rental housing, company stores, churches, and Sunday schools. Some fathers worked in skilled and supervisory positions in the mills, others in construction or on village farms. At least until the early 1830s, mill village mothers mainly cared for the family, carried out endless household chores, tended the family garden, and took in boarders. The village families' young children, adolescent boys and girls, and unmarried young daughters continued to be the Slater mills' main workforce. The Rhode Island system relied on the family authority of fathers to supply the mills with a disciplined workforce. The yarn that the Slater-type mills produced was either sold to merchants or distributed to farm women for weaving into cloth. By the time of his death in 1835, Slater owned or held an interest in thirteen mills in three states in southern New England.

In 1810 the merchant Frances Cabot Lowell left Boston for a two-year tour of English and Scottish textile mills. He was especially interested in integrating into one large-scale mechanized mill all the processes – carding, spinning, and weaving – used in making affordable cloth. With a capital funding of $400,000, Lowell joined his close friend Nathan Appleton in founding the Boston Manufacturing Company. Drawing on the valuable assistance of a mechanic, Paul Moody, the company constructed its first textile mill on the Charles River at Waltham, Massachusetts. Mills built under what became known as the Waltham, or Lowell, system were ten times larger than the average Slater-type mill and incorporated power looms. Unlike the Slater mills, which were managed either by Slater himself or by a member of his family, the proprietors of the Lowell mills were absentee owners; day-to-day management was left to hired agents. But the most telling difference between the two systems of textile production lay in the nature of the workforce. In contrast to the Slater mills, which relied on the labor of children, Lowell mills mostly employed adult, single young women, who were recruited from the surrounding New England countryside. Appalled by the social and economic conditions that he had observed in English industrial cities like Manchester, Lowell believed that a manufacturing

Figure 2.4 A view of cotton mills at Lowell, Massachusetts, in 1852. Hand-colored wood engraving. "View of Boott Cotton Mills at Lowell, Massachusetts," from *Gleason's Pictorial* (Boston, 1852). Courtesy of American Textile History Museum, Lowell, MA.

system should be fashioned in the United States that took into account the health, character, and well-being of the workforce. Thus the women of the Lowell mills lived in carefully monitored boardinghouses that were intended to reassure their parents that millwork was safe and respectable. The system was an immense success, and by 1836 about twenty mills, valued at more than $6 million and employing some 6,800 workers, lined the canals of Lowell, Massachusetts.

That Frances Lowell provided his female employees with a respectable work and living environment only partially explains the attraction that working in the mills held for single young women throughout rural New England. Using the records of the Hamilton Manufacturing Company, a Lowell-type mill, the historian Thomas Dublin, in *Women at Work: The Transformation of Work and Community in Lowell, Massachusetts, 1826–1860*, found that the women who worked in the company's mills were typically between the ages of fifteen and thirty, unmarried, and living in a company-owned boardinghouse. Most of them were from farming families; very few were foreign born. Why did they come to the mills? One way to answer this question is to look at the economic standing of their families. Based on his review of local property records, Dublin determined that the fathers of most of the women who worked for the Hamilton Company owned property that placed them in the middle ranks of wealth in their hometowns. Thus the money that these women earned was not needed to support their families. Instead, these workingwomen spent their pay on self-education or on new, more sophisticated clothing; some set aside the money for their dowries. "Lowell Girls" married a bit later (although at the same general rate) than was the norm at the time and were unlikely to return to live in the countryside that they had left behind. For them, mill work presented a route to a different and more independent way of life, one that they seem to have fully embraced.

Figure 2.5   December 1845 cover page of the *Lowell Offering*, a magazine written by female textile operatives in Lowell, Massachusetts, "to show what factory girls had the power to do." In it, the women portrayed themselves and their work in a dignified light. Courtesy of American Textile History Museum, Lowell, MA.

Cultural Response to Industrialization

The Slater and especially the Lowell mills best approximate the definition of the early English factory system offered in the mid-1830s by Andrew Ure, a chemist and student of the British textile industry. Ure described factories as "the combined operations of many orders of work people, adult and young, in tending with assiduous skill a series of productive machines continuously impelled by a central power." More than just a series of economic and technological changes, industrialization challenged accepted social and cultural assumptions and required people to reconsider how they looked at the world. Whether seen in the new factories or in the diverse workplaces found in cities and towns throughout

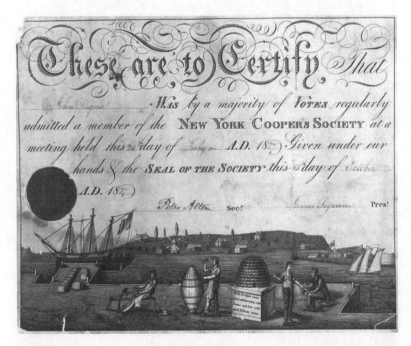

Figure 2.6   A membership certificate for the New York Coopers Society in the mid-1820s. Line engraving, ca. 1825; 9 1/2 × 11 7/8 in. (image #59482). Courtesy of New-York Historical Society.

the United States, industrialization placed a high value on continuous and constant effort. As Paul Faler has noted in *Mechanics and Manufacturers in the Early Industrial Revolution: Lynn, Massachusetts, 1780–1860,* an industrial work ethic based on diligence and systematic labor required both moral discipline and the alteration of customs and traditions that would interfere with productive labor. Industrial morality placed a high value on individual character as exhibited through sober, thrifty industrial work habits. To encourage the formation of an industrial work ethic among their workers, businessmen in the 1820s and after introduced new associations and organizations, such as the Society for the Promotion of Industry, Frugality and Temperance, which was established in Lynn in 1826.

For their part, workers responded to the new industrial system in a variety of ways. Labor historians have cited three types of

Figure 2.7 A banner displayed by housewrights during an 1841 parade in Portland, Maine, sponsored by the Maine Charitable Mechanic Association. Painted cloth; item #36611. Collections of the Maine Historical Society.

Figure 2.8   A banner displayed by blacksmiths during an 1841 parade in Portland, Maine, sponsored by the Maine Charitable Mechanic Association. On the reverse is the slogan "Strike While the Iron Is Hot." Painted cloth; item #36610. Collections of the Maine Historical Society.

responses: traditionalist, loyalist or revivalist, and radical or rebel. Although there is ample evidence that each of these responses took hold among different groups of workers, their reactions also reflected more than one of these ideal types. The traditional worker persisted in maintaining time-honored customs and habits, especially those associated with rural America. Usually males who were young, unmarried, and unskilled, traditionalists worked and lived hard. Their libertine habits made them the frequent objects of reform efforts. Although uninterested in radical ideals and theories, traditionalists resisted employers' efforts to remake them and frequently united with other workers to seek higher wages. Loyalist or revivalist workers, both male and female, extolled the virtues of the new industrial work ethic either out of a fundamental belief in its correctness or, sometimes, from a sense that appearing to adopt the modern habits was in their best interest.

Moreover, religion, especially the popular revivals led by Charles Grandison Finney in the early 1830s, also promoted personal responsibility and self-discipline, thus reinforcing values compatible with the industrial work ethic. Yet religious ideals could also form the basis for a stinging critique of the competitive individualism that was embraced by the rising businessmen of the industrial era.

Radicals or rebels offered the most organized resistance to the new industrial order. During the second and third decades of the nineteenth century, workers in New York, Philadelphia, and other industrial cities, as well as the so-called Lowell Girls, formed unions or associations and engaged in strikes and protests intended to protect their status in the workplace and to advance their material well-being. Simultaneously, they also fashioned workingmen's parties and political movements that sought such reforms as the abolition of imprisonment for debt; the end of the prison contract labor system; the creation of free, common school educational systems; and, especially, the reduction of the workday to ten hours. By insisting that the government protect and advance the interests of the "producing classes," the labor movement of the 1820s and 1830s offered a radical alternative to what workers feared would otherwise result in their being reduced to the status of what they called "wage slaves."

A work ethic that emphasized diligent effort challenged the more irregular work habits long practiced by Americans who worked on farms or in artisan craft shops. Before industrialization little distinction had been made between work and play. Drink and the sociability of the neighborhood tavern or of the even less respectable grog shop had been a mainstay of traditional work culture. Even with industrialization, a relatively casual pace of work persisted well into the nineteenth century. In Lynn, shoemakers insisted that their employers provide them with a half pint of liquor each day as part of their wages. "Treating time," when the communal jug was passed around, was part of the accepted afternoon routine at many workplaces in Philadelphia. A ship's carpenter working in a New York shipyard describes the arrival of Aunt Arlie McVane at half past eight in the morning offering for sale crullers, donuts, and a variety of sweets from her baskets "until every man and boy, bosses and all, in the yard, had been supplied." She was followed by Johnnie Gogean, an English candyman, at half past ten; after him "there was a general sailing out of the yard and into the convenient grog-shops after whiskey." In the afternoon, Uncle Jack Gridder supplied a cake lunch, and at about five o'clock Johnnie made a second appearance. Old World customs persisted. Irish outworkers and unskilled laborers in Philadelphia in the 1820s and 1830s continued to celebrate St. Monday, a day to recover from the rigors of a pub life on Sunday that was spent running foot races and playing games in the city's streets.

Holding onto the Familiar

During the 1820s and 1830s, traditionalist workers resisted manu-facturers' efforts to assert the bosses' presumed moral authority. In contrast to the more organized opposition identified with their radical brothers and sisters, traditionalists demonstrated their defiance by staying aloof from the manufacturers' attempts to reform them. For example, in the early nineteenth century, as the historian Bruce Laurie has noted, the volunteer fire companies found in cities throughout the northern states also functioned as vital social outlets for recreation and camaraderie. Highly competitive rival companies of volunteers rushed to fires and frequently engaged in fights at the site to determine which company would actually put out the fire. Employers condemned the rowdiness and lamented the time that their journeymen spent loafing in the firehouses rather than working. Manufacturers' efforts to replace the volunteers with professionals in these years proved unavailing.

Neighborhood militia companies also became important sources of group identity. Training day was more a social occasion, more a time for drinking, than it was a time for learning military maneuvers. Also, in cities like New York, journeymen and apprentices formed gangs that took their names from the workers' neighborhoods, like the Broadway Boys, or from their employment, like the butchers' gang known as the Hide-Binders. At times in northern cities, the traditionalists' "us versus them" mentality led to mob violence against free blacks, whom the Irish and other white workers accused of being competitors for their jobs.

Traditionalist resistance to adopting the cultural values of industrializing America was expressed not only through collective activities but also through the voluntary acts of individuals. Although there is evidence of only one organized strike in the Slater mills prior to 1840, workers nevertheless expressed their discontent in a number of ways. One precipitating factor was the change in the composition of the workforce as the size and scale of the Slater mills grew. For example, by the early 1830s, the population of Merino Village, a manufacturing compound built in 1812 in Dudley, Massachusetts, had increased from 60 to 108 workers; of these, only 33 percent were attached to families. As the company's agents tried to assert greater discipline over the workers, incidents of arson and machine vandalism appear in the records. In sabotaging their machines, Slater workers seem to have acted less from an inclination to destroy the mills than from a desire to provide themselves with a respite from the speedup of their work. Another, less violent, means by which workers demonstrated their resistance to factory work pressures was by simply failing to turn up for work. Attendance records in 1830 for operatives at the Slater and Merino Village mills indicate that they were absent for about 15 percent of their working hours. Finally, disgruntled mill workers could simply quit. Voluntary departures among Slater employees rose from about 50 percent of the workforce in 1820 to more than 120 percent in 1840 (a worker would leave, be replaced, and then the replacement would leave). Even when the Slater workers appear to have accepted the new time discipline, they sought ways to modify the regimen to meet their needs. For example, mill workers living in Merino Village in the 1830s who accepted longer hours began to insist that any additional work they did be purchased with extra pay. It was through these kinds of largely passive but sometimes more aggressive actions that traditionalist workers demonstrated their independence.

Religion, the Revivalists, and the New Work Ethic

In *Democracy in America* (two volumes, 1835 and 1840), the account of his visit to the United States in the early 1830s, the French political thinker and historian Alexis de Tocqueville cited the formation of "civil associations," that is, voluntary organizations, as a particularly distinctive feature of democracy in America. Such groups were intended to transmit the values that the leading citizens in their communities held dear. During these same years, the United States also experienced what historians refer to as the Second Great Awakening, a period of intense religious fervor. Therefore, it is not surprising that members of the elite, including leading manufacturers, created new religious and civil associations to promote those habits and values that they saw as compatible with industrial morality, as well as to combat those that they believed were not. In particular, during the 1820s and 1830s the issue of temperance became a focal point of employers' campaigns to remake the workforce. Rochester, a town that, as we have seen, grew rapidly in the wake of the Erie Canal's completion, offers a compelling example of how this process worked.

Even before Finney brought his revival movement to Rochester in November 1830, the city's manufacturers and masters had come together to stop the drunken and rowdy behavior of the workers in their mills and shops. It would appear that the owners' recognition of what they had come to see as a growing menace had taken place almost overnight. There were still no temperance organizations in Rochester as late as 1825, and it remained, as we have seen, a common practice for masters to treat their journeymen from a bottle they kept in the shop for that purpose. But, as Rochester's economy boomed and manufacturing became concentrated in larger establishments, and as the locus of work shifted to outside the home, the divide between the new merchant entrepreneurs and the journeymen widened. Drink was now seen by the proprietors as a social problem to be fixed by reforming workmen's personal habits. In 1828 these worried gentlemen formed the Rochester Society for the Promotion of Temperance. Relying initially on moral suasion, on the power of their example and position within the community, they hoped to encourage the workingmen to abstain voluntarily. These reform efforts failed. In the neighborhoods where the workers lived some 100 licensed local bars continued to dispense nearly 200,000 gallons of whiskey annually, and church membership was falling dramatically.

Recognizing that voluntary methods were not working, Rochester's businessmen sought to build on the religious enthusiasm that greeted Finney's revival. In 1832 the city's wealthy evangelicals started the Free Presbyterian Church to minister among canal workers, transients, and Rochester's unchurched poor. The year before, they had founded the Rochester Savings Bank to encourage thrift and personal discipline among the city's working class. An even more direct approach, the rewarding of evidence of right behavior, also appears to have been used by the city's business leaders. What Paul Johnson refers to as "sponsored mobility," that is, steady work and economic advancement, was a reward often given to the churchgoing members in the workforce. As was common in most communities in nineteenth-century America, Rochester experienced a high population turnover in these years. But, as Johnson found, the more successful workmen in Rochester were those who were less transient and went to church. Rochester's churchgoing clerks were twice as likely as their non-churchgoing peers to remain in the city, and churchgoing laborers were three-and-a-half times as likely as non-churchgoing laborers to stay. Indeed, between 1827 and 1837, two-thirds of the laborers who joined churches and remained in Rochester improved their occupational standing.

Johnson views the impact of evangelism from the top down, that is, as a means by which Rochester's businessmen were able to impose the character-building values that they saw as necessary to create an industrious and disciplined labor force. Yet, in a path-breaking essay on Protestantism and the American labor movement, the historian Herbert Gutman observed that the Gilded Age trade unionists, labor reformers, and radicals themselves drew on an antebellum evangelical tradition that "offered a religious sanction for *their* discontent with industrial laissez faire and 'Acquisitive Man.'" Building on Gutman's insight, the historian Jama Lazerow reveals how evangelical religion not only promoted the employers' aspirations for "social control" but also furnished the labor movement with a language of resistance that helped workers "make sense of [their] rapidly changing lives." To see workers only as the "tools" of the new middle-class entrepreneurs and the evangelical churches is to ignore this more radical dynamic.

In *Religion and the Working Class in Antebellum America*, Lazerow examines labor radicals' involvement with the church in a number of New England communities, as well as in Wilmington, Delaware, in the Mid-Atlantic region, and in Rochester in upstate New York. Self-consciously Christian, Rochester's labor activists expressed a faith that "religion shall sustain the just." This religious impulse, which employers in the canal city had relied on to tame the "excitability" of the working people of Rochester, also stimulated the first stirrings of organized labor unrest. In one example, as housing construction boomed in the city in the early 1830s, merchant capitalists and their subcontractors pushed local carpenters, joiners, and other building tradesmen to work from dawn to dusk. In an effort to resist, the carpenters organized a union, the Journeymen Carpenters' and Joiners' Society (JCJS), and, in 1834, "pledged themselves to the 'TEN-HOUR SYSTEM.'" Not only did a steward of the First Methodist Church lead the strike but, as Lazerow found, the officers of the JCJS and some ninety-one signers of the strike announcement were also church members. Similarly, Henry Church Frink, the principal editor of the *Working-Man's Advocate*, a daily newspaper published by the Rochester Typographical Association, was a supporter of Bible classes and Sabbath schools and regularly quoted scripture. Believing that he lived in a "Christian community," Frink condemned greed as the bane of society and called for a morality built on "genuine charity." For Lazerow, religion should be understood not just as a tool to bring about workers' submission but also as a source of inspiration for the developing labor movement.

In communities throughout the United States, a reform movement developed in the 1820s and 1830s that relied on both moral suasion and legal coercion to promote and enforce acceptable standards of conduct. In Lynn in these years, as has been noted, the Society for the Promotion of Industry, Frugality and Temperance took up the cause of total abstinence. Businessmen were exhorted to ban liquor from their homes and workplaces and to hire only those workers who did not use "ardent spirits." In Philadelphia, Albert Barnes, a Presbyterian minister and Finney's local counterpart, preached individual responsibility and temperance and celebrated industrialism. As they had for Rochester, historians have discerned in Philadelphia an association between evangelical morality and worldly success. More than half of Philadelphia's Presbyterians and Methodists who started as journeymen in the early 1830s had become either master craftsmen or small retailers by the 1850s. In New York City, temperance was once again at the forefront of businessmen's efforts to remake the city's labor force.

By the 1830s the keeping of St. Monday appears to have faded in the city. Efforts among New York's workingmen themselves to promote abstinence culminated in 1840 in the founding of a local group, the Washingtonian Temperance Society. In less than a year, the society claimed a membership of more than 20,000 men (members included petty entrepreneurs and master craftsmen as well as journeymen and unskilled laborers) pledged against drink. Washingtonians fought their war against the evils of drink by fostering nonalcoholic sociability among the members and by providing those in need with assistance such as food and clothing. Members of the Lynn Washington Society in Massachusetts signed a pledge of total abstinence; rather than simply condemn drinkers, members testified to their own struggles with demon rum.

There appears to have been a certain ambivalence in the revivalists' protestations of faith. One worker in Rochester was quoted as saying in 1836 about his church attendance, "I don't give a d—n. I get five dollars more in a month than before I got religion." As already mentioned, becoming a church member may have reflected an outward accommodation to the practical realities of the workplace rather than a fundamental change of heart. Other workers, however, clearly rejected the call to change their "immoral" ways. Open resistance to the moralizers' appeals to working people to remake their personal habits took two forms. Many workers simply maintained their libertine lifestyle. Drink and the social customs surrounding it proved impervious to the evangelicals' efforts to curb unproductive behavior. Union meetings continued to be held in taverns and hotel bars, and drinking on the job persisted. But revivalist workers also could, and did, avail themselves of religious values that were intended to transform them into a more hard-working and docile labor force for their own ends, by using them as texts for advocating labor's rights. For example, Rochester's churchgoing workers, including two Methodist leaders, one of whom was a lay exhorter, supported the local carpenters' movement in the 1830s to win a ten-hour workday. A Rochester labor paper, the *Spirit of the Age*, advocated labor's demands and called for workers to receive those privileges that "a wise and beneficent Providence saw fit to bestow." Nevertheless, a much more secular radicalism also inspired many leaders of the labor movement in the 1820s and 1830s.

Radical Resistance to the New Industrial Order

What historians call "the first true American labor movement" was born in Philadelphia in 1827 when the skilled workers in the city's craft societies came together to organize the Mechanics' Union of Trade Associations (MUTA). The following year, the MUTA supported the carpenters' successful campaign to establish a ten-hour workday in their shops. Subsequently, the MUTA decided to enter politics, launching the Philadelphia Working Men's Party "to promote the interests and enlightenment of the working classes." Also in 1828, the New York Working Men's Party was organized at a meeting of mechanics called to resist the imposition of an eleven-hour workday. The assembled workers appointed a "Committee of Fifty," which, in the fall, presented a slate of candidates for New York's State Assembly and Senate. Workers' entry into politics to achieve their economic goals, as well as their unity across craft lines, distinguished the labor movement in the late 1820s through the mid-1830s.

In more than sixty communities throughout the United States, workingmen's political movements united behind a common platform during these years. Workers condemned laws that they claimed bestowed special privileges on an emerging class-bound aristocracy. To defend their status as independent citizens in a democratic republic, workingmen and their allies called for the replacement of "pauper schools" with a free, tax-supported common school educational system; the abolition of imprisonment for debt; the prohibition of licensed monopolies; and an end to prison contract labor. They also insisted that new laws be passed, including mechanics' lien laws, to protect the wages of workingmen. "Equal Universal Education" headed the list of reforms in almost every labor newspaper. Citing evidence that more than 24,000 children between the ages of five and fifteen in New York City had no schooling and that an equal number attended charity schools, workers condemned the educational system of the day for undermining equal opportunity. The workingmen's agenda also emphasized local concerns. The New England Association, reflecting its agrarian composition, demanded the reform of land tenure laws, whereas, not surprising for an urban group, the Working Men of Boston expressed concern over the privileges of elite professionals and advocated for a reduction in the fees that professionals charged.

A number of radical labor theorists nurtured the workingmen's movement. Early on, the New York Working Men's Party reflected the influence of Thomas Skidmore, a machinist and the author of *The Rights of Man to Property!* (1829). Skidmore denounced all laws that perpetuated the "hereditary transmission of wealth" and looked to political action as a means of ensuring "equal property to all adults." In Philadelphia, William Heighton was a founder of the MUTA and the editor of the group's official organ, the *Mechanics' Free Press*, the nation's first labor newspaper. His views, like those of Skidmore, reveal the influence of the labor theory of value, the doctrine that all wealth is derived from labor. For Heighton, because the producer was the source of all wealth, the whole product of his labor was owed him. Competition, or the struggle to undersell, was, according to Heighton, inherent in capitalism and inevitably rewarded the "avaricious accumulators and ungenerous employers" at the expense of honorable masters or producers. Heighton identified monopolistic or aristocratic legislation as the source of labor's exploitation. According to such proponents of the labor theory of value as Skidmore and Heighton, the inequities of the present system would be addressed only once the poor and other "friends of equal rights" united to gain control of government through the election of candidates for public office who supported the interests of the working classes.

As already noted for Rochester, labor activists often found inspiration in scripture for their critique of emerging capitalist social relationships. Heighton exhorted Philadelphia's reforming clergy not only to "'teach evangelical truths' but also to call for 'the absolute necessity of undeviating justice between man and man.'" It was the duty of the "'the legislative, judicial, and theological classes' to exercise 'their influence to remedy [the workers'] degraded condition.'" For Heighton, here lay "the proper role of religion," as the historian Ronald Schultz has pointed out, "in a future republic of labor." The message of evangelical religion for the working class was not just one of submission and self-denial. Heighton invoked a more communal vision of America, one in which America is a just democratic economic order realized in a system of equal rights.

The goals outlined in the platforms of the various working-men's parties and the parties' clear denunciation of monopoly and defense of small-scale production all resonated with Jacksonian artisans and mechanics. Workingmen's parties ran lively election campaigns. Their rallies attracted crowds who listened as speakers attacked the existing social order and extolled the virtues of the producing classes. In the 1829 election in New York for the state legislature, the Working Men's Party polled 6,000 votes out of 21,000 cast, although only one of its candidates won. Also in 1829, the Working Men's Party in Philadelphia garnered three times the vote it had polled the previous year, some 30 percent of the total vote. Nevertheless, the workers' turn to electoral politics proved to be fleeting; within two years, workingmen's parties had largely disappeared. Inexperience, inadequate organization, and factional discord among the parties' leaders, as well as the willingness of the major political parties to embrace (co-opt) aspects of the labor parties' program, such as debtor relief and even reduced hours, were among the reasons for the collapse of workers' first experiments in electoral politics.

As the workingmen departed the field of politics, trade union-led economic actions intensified, especially on behalf of the ten-hour day. About a quarter of the 172 recorded turnouts (strikes) between 1833 and 1837 revolved around the issue of hours. Labor historians note that one of the most frequent causes of complaint among working people was their lack of leisure time. Radical mechanics and artisans agreed with William Heighton that only after workers had secured sufficient time for self-education would they be able to defend their equal rights. In his famous 1835 "Ten-Hour Circular," Seth Luther, a Rhode Island carpenter and labor activist, condemned the incipient "tyrannical system" that compelled the mechanic to labor to exhaustion. He called on workingmen to defend their rights as "American Citizens," just as their forefathers had in the "War of the Revolution."

"From Six to Six" became the rallying cry in Philadelphia in 1835 for the coal heavers. Rather than continue to work the more traditional schedule of sunrise to sunset, which often meant fourteen-hour workdays during the summer months, the men who moved coal, especially on and off ships, demanded a twelve-hour workday that included an hour off for breakfast and another hour off for lunch. The employers' decision to hire replacement coal workers ignited the nation's first general strike, which was reported to eventually include some 20,000 workers in the City of Brotherly Love. To Philadelphia's employers, the hours issue was a matter of the natural order of the free market. The "law" of competition or self-interest could not, they insisted, be flouted by any combination or union among the workers. Striking workers countered that the benefits of labor should go to the creators of wealth rather than to those who would tyrannize over them. Ten hours, they declared, was consistent with the natural order. The ten-hour idea spread to communities large and small throughout the Northeast, often, as in Philadelphia, meeting with great success.

Beginning in 1833, a surging labor movement engaged in extralocal and collective actions. Specific trades organized nationwide unions. In 1835 the printers founded the National Typographical Society, and other craft unions soon followed their example. Before this, citywide labor federations known as General Trades' Unions (GTUs) were launched in New York and Philadelphia, and in more than a dozen other cities throughout the Northeast. Local GTUs provided assistance for workers on strike in 1834 for higher wages and improved conditions in Poughkeepsie, New York; New York City; Newark; Boston; and Philadelphia. Between 1833 and 1836, nearly half of the forty strikes that apparently took place in New York in the leading trades were coordinated by the GTU. Philadelphia's GTU, which brought together fifty-three local unions and totaled more than 10,000 members, developed a highly structured organization that included five executive officers elected semiannually; two deliberative bodies, the General Assembly and the Finance Committee; and a profusion of elective and appointive committees. When a delegation of striking Philadelphia bookbinders appealed for support from the New York GTU in February 1836, the New York organization passed a resolution calling on its members to support "their fellow mechanics" who were standing up for their rights "against aristocratical tyranny." Financial support was also sent to the Philadelphia bookbinders from unions in Albany; Newark; Washington, DC; and Baltimore.

Ten hours was an important issue for the GTUs and was a leading objective of the first attempt to establish a nationwide federation of unions, the National Trades' Union (NTU). A national call in the summer of 1834 for citywide trade associations to send delegates to meet in New York City led to the formation of the NTU. The new national union, which held conventions in each of the next two years, functioned mainly as a forum for trade unions and as a promoter of the labor platform of the 1820s, especially for education reform. In 1835 the NTU came to the aid of mechanics employed by the federal government who were seeking a ten-hour day. In response to an appeal from the NTU, President Andrew Jackson established the ten-hour day in naval yards in those cities where this workday was the accepted standard. Desirous, however, of a "more permanent solution" that could be won without unceasing and costly strikes, the NTU endorsed cooperative production. The NTU hoped that, by owning and operating their own places of work, mechanics could reverse their loss of control over their labor. Such collective effort was needed if workers were ever to obtain the "full product" of their labor.

The mid-1830s also witnessed the formation of a radical agenda among the women who went to work in the Lowell mills. During the 1820s, as new textile mills were constructed throughout New England, competition in the industry intensified and mill owners tried to cut costs by reducing the wages they paid to their women workers. In 1834, even before mill agents had posted the notices of wage cuts at the Lowell mills, the workers held meetings and organized support for their cause from throughout the mill community. An alleged leader was soon dismissed, and 800 women went out on strike in response. Declaring that "UNION IS POWER," they announced that, as "daughters of freemen still," they would resist "[t]he oppressing hand of avarice [that] would enslave us." The turnout did not last long, and the protesters were unable to reverse the proposed wage reductions. Nevertheless, by going out on strike, the women had shown themselves willing to act collectively in ways that breached commonly accepted assumptions about female propriety.

Two years later, the Lowell women went out on strike again. In October 1836 their newly organized Factory Girls' Association, with a membership of 2,500, coordinated a second turnout among the women operatives in Lowell. This time, management had announced an increase in boardinghouse rates, which, since these costs were deducted from the workers' pay, amounted to much the same thing as a wage cut. Once again, the women proclaimed that, as the daughters of men who had refused to "wear the [British] yoke," they were determined to resist wage cuts that threatened their economic independence. The 1836 turnout lasted longer than the first. More than 1,500 operatives went out on strike, almost twice the number in 1834. The Lowell women were also more successful this time, for the company apparently rescinded the room-and-board increases.

The textile workers of Lowell would not be the only women caught up in the labor militancy of the 1820s and 1830s. After the War of 1812, especially in the garment trades in New York and other commercial cities in the United States, the outwork system provided job opportunities for women working as seamstresses and "tailoresses." In 1810, in Philadelphia, the political economist Mathew Carey pronounced the "low rate of of female labor" a "grievance of the very first magnitude." Carey observed that men earned "five, six, seven dollars a week" whereas "female labour" was paid "only a dollar" or so "for similar, or nearly similar" work, which left the women facing two narrow choices, "STARVATION OR POLLUTION." In 1829 Carey established a $100 gold medal "for the best essay on the inadequacy of wages paid to seamstresses, spinners, shoebinders &c." The winning essay, by Joseph Tuckerman, a Unitarian minister in Boston and an advocate of reform, asserted that seamstresses' low wages were a national problem with alarming social consequences.

In the 1820s and 1830s women laboring as outworkers in the urban garment trades took the initiative to improve their condition. The historian Christine Stansell has noted that in 1825 seamstresses in New York conducted the first all-women's strike in the United States. Six years later the tailoresses of that city turned out to enforce a price list. Rejecting the accepted view of women as submissive, the tailoresses infused their labor activism with a militant feminism. One activist, Sarah Monroe, pointed out that "It needs no small share of courage for us who have been used to impositions and oppression from our youth" to defend "our own rights," and she asked why the women, unlike the men, should "bear oppression in silence." Likewise, a speaker at the first meeting of the Tailoresses Society attributed the workingwomen's difficulties with their employers to, as Stansell noted, women's "subordination in *all* social relations." Even as the strike appeared to be failing in its second month, Monroe insisted that "If we do not come forth in our own defence, what will become of us? ... Long have the poor tailoresses of this city borne their oppression in silence; until *patience* is no longer a virtue." Although the strike ended shortly thereafter, and the Tailoresses Society folded, a commitment to female self-reliance lived on.

In May 1830 twenty-two anonymous "ladies of respectability and intelligence" circulated a petition in Baltimore stating that the wages of the city's seamstresses "was entirely inadequate to their support" and that there needed to be found some means "of remedy, or at least of mitigation of their sufferings." The petition, the historian Seth Rockman shows, was part of a growing national conversation that made the seamstresses' wages "a matter of both Christian morality and secular political economy." In Baltimore a women-run charity, the Humane Impartial Society, offered poor seamstresses piecework at a rate 50 percent above the prevailing market rates. In fact, Mathew Carey was so impressed by their effort that in 1831 he dedicated a major publication on women's wages, *Address to the Wealthy of the Land*, to the organization. One local supporter, a lawyer, Ebenezer L. Finley, celebrated the society for "dispensing, not charity but work; and by requiting the poor widow for her labor with *living* wages."

Philanthropy alone, Rockman notes, was not able to "guarantee economic competency to Baltimore's seamstresses." One problem was the sheer size of the need: only one-tenth of the 1,600 women who applied to the society for sewing in 1830 could be offered work. In September 1833, as part of a growing labor movement in Baltimore that included establishing a general trades organization and had elected two mechanics to the Maryland legislature, the city's seamstresses organized themselves into the Female Union Society. Hoping to establish a standard bill of wages, a large number of seamstresses met in Fells Point and resolved to "enter into a positive agreement to take out no work from the shops until proper rates shall be established." Their cause quickly gained the support of a local newspaper, the *Baltimore America*, which, having noted that the Humane Impartial Society paid the women "18 3/4¢" for the shirts and pants they made, declared that surely "the prosperous merchant tailors could do the same." The strike began on October 1, 1833.

The city's clothing manufacturers immediately met in a local coffeehouse and agreed to make a counteroffer to the striking women of a 25 percent increase. The seamstresses celebrated their victory as giving "*Industry its* DUE REWARD." Yet some of the employers who signed the official price of the Female Union Society expected to abandon it at the first opportunity. Their plan was apparently foiled when the society published the names of the manufacturers who had signed the agreement and those who had not. According to Rockman, one of those intending to pull out instead "blew the whistle" on the scheme. After the strike, however, the society virtually disappears from the public record. Moreover, an 1835 survey of piece rates paid to seamstresses in Baltimore indicates that they were being paid rates far below the 1833 standard. In subsequent years, many seamstresses found themselves the object of poor relief.

The nationwide financial panic of 1837 cut short the labor militancy of the mid-1830s. Innumerable businesses failed, and many manufacturing firms closed. The severe economic downturn in the aftermath of the panic resulted in the disbanding of recently organized national trade unions, along with the citywide associations and the NTU. With the ranks of the unemployed swelling, working Americans had little choice but to accept whatever wage was offered them. Faced by a new round of wage cuts between 1837 and 1843, the workingwomen in Lowell could offer little resistance. Race riots erupted in many urban areas in the North, when mobs of unemployed white workers took out their frustration by rampaging through the cities' African American ghettos. The growing number of immigrants led to the formation of nativist political associations and fraternal societies that splintered working-class unity. The class organizations and achievements of the Jacksonian worker proved to be ephemeral. Yet the basic objectives of these groups and the growing sense of disaffection that the labor movement articulated remained as a legacy of the 1820s and 1830s.

CHAPTER THREE

The Industrial Worker in Free Labor America

Lynn as a Microcosm

On Washington's Birthday, February 22, 1860, the Journeymen Cordwainers' Mutual Benefit Society in Lynn, Massachusetts, went out on strike. Members of the Cordwainers' Society, which had been organized two years before, pledged to withhold their labor until their employers agreed to sign the "bill of prices," or wage list, that the workers had submitted to them. In the months leading up to the strike, the society prepared both by creating a special police force to maintain discipline and to keep order during the walkout and by sending agents throughout the state to urge all shoemakers to strike for the same bill of wages. Eventually, the walkout would involve some 20,000 shoe workers, or about half their total number in Massachusetts. Unlike earlier, more spontaneous, turnouts by small groups of workers, the Great Strike of 1860 was a modern strike, as the historian Paul Faler has noted, the culmination of two years of concerted effort and planning.

The Dawning of American Labor: The New Republic to the Industrial Age, First Edition. Brian Greenberg.
© 2018 John Wiley & Sons, Inc. Published 2018 by John Wiley & Sons, Inc.

The 1860 strike marked a turning point in the decades of changes that reshaped the shoe industry in Lynn and its environs. A cordwainer in the early eighteenth century, engaged in what was called a "bespoke" trade, made the entire shoe for an individual customer. By the mid-1830s, however, although shoes and boots were still manufactured in the workers' homes or in artisan shops, most production in Lynn took place in central shops (unmechanized workshops where the leather was cut and the boots and shoes were finished), dramatically increasing output. Producing boots and shoes for what was now a national market, slightly more than 5,000 Lynn journeymen cordwainers turned out two and a half million pairs of shoes valued at more than $1.5 million. Two decades later, in the 1850s, shoes and boots were more commonly assembled in factories, and the output of Lynn's shoe industry reached nine million pairs valued at more than $4 million. Whereas the city's largest shoe-manufacturing firms controlled nearly one-third of the total workforce in 1850, some 200 shoe bosses – double the number in the mid-thirties – employed more than one-half of the workforce by the time of the 1860 strike.

Shoemakers continued to work with the same tools and to apply the same techniques that their parents and grandparents had used even as production was being reorganized in the first half of the nineteenth century. Mechanization became a factor in shoe and boot production when manufacturers in 1852 successfully adapted the Howe sewing machine to the stitching of shoe leather, transforming the shoe-binding process. Before then, women working at home would bind (sew) the upper parts of the shoe by hand; males did the lasting (shaping the upper and the inner sole to size) and bottoming (fastening the sole, heel, and upper together). A family economy prevailed that included the earnings of the female binders. The new sewing machines, although at first powered manually, dramatically increased the output of the shoe binders and created a new class of factory-based "machine girls."

Figure 3.1   The bottoming room of the shoe manufacturer B. F. Spinney and Company in Lynn, Massachusetts, in the early 1870s. From Horace Greeley et al., *The Great Industries of the United States: Being an Historical Summary of the Origin, Growth, and Perfection of the Chief Industrial Arts of This Country* (Hartford, CT: J. B. Burr, 1872), p. 1253.

According to the 1860 US census, the boot and shoe industry in Lynn was "assuming the character of the factory system."

In 1860 the Journeymen Cordwainers' Society fought not only against wage cuts and centralized production but also for the right of shoe workers to set their own price for their labor and in defense of the customary family wage system. On March 7, in one key workers' demonstration during the strike, thousands of Lynn journeymen and female binders marched together, accompanied by local fire companies, militia units, cornet bands, neighbors, and friends. A sketch of the event in *Frank Leslie's Illustrated Newspaper* captures the stirring scene: flanking Willard F. Oliver, the chief marshal, who represented the men's strike committee, are rows of women marchers, some of whom carry a banner that proclaims, "American Ladies Will Not Be Slaves / Give Us a Fair Compensation and We Labour Cheerfully."

Figure 3.2   Lady shoemakers' procession during the Great Strike of 1860, in Lynn, Massachusetts. From *Frank Leslie's Illustrated Newspaper*, March 17, 1860. Courtesy of American Social History Project.

This demonstration has always been viewed as a symbol of the strikers' unity. Yet the female homeworkers who marched in the parade spurned the appeal of the machine girls, who were demanding increased pay for all binders. Instead, the female home binders in the "Great Procession" joined with each other, explaining that "[w]eak in physical strength but strong in moral courage we dare to battle for the right, shoulder to shoulder with our fathers, husbands, and brothers." In 1860 family solidarity triumphed over sisterhood.

The shoe workers in Lynn in 1860 saw themselves as the bearers of an equal rights tradition. Based on the ideals of the first American Revolution, the notion that all Americans shared an equal right to wealth and power lay at the core of the principles espoused by labor radicals throughout the first half of the nineteenth century. The "Cordwainers' Song," composed by the local poet and historian Alonzo Lewis, became the strikers' anthem:

> Shoemakers of Lynn, be brave!
> Renew your resolves again;
> Sink not to the state of slave,
> But stand for rights like men!
> ...
>
> The workman is worthy [of] his hire,
> No tyrant shall hold us in thrall;
> ...
>
> We shall triumph by justice and right,
> For like men we'll hold onto the last!

Two distinct classes had emerged in the Lynn shoe industry: a small group of shoe bosses – the merchant entrepreneurs

Figure 3.3   Upheaval in the streets of Lynn, Massachusetts, during the Great Strike of 1860. From *Frank Leslie's Illustrated Newspaper*, March 17, 1860. Everett Collection Inc / Alamy stock photo.

who bought the raw materials, owned the critical means of production, and sold the finished product – and a much larger group – the workers who labored solely for wages. Headlines in the newspapers of the day proclaimed the strike to be a "Rebellion among Workmen of New England" and the "Beginning of Conflict between Capital and Labor." Nevertheless, by early April the strike was failing. First the female machine binders abandoned the strike, and then the male shoemakers also began returning to work. In 1860 the lack of unity among the strikers and the impact of mechanization had given the manufacturers the upper hand.

Not Just Lynn

Before 1860, comparable, if less dramatic, changes than those in shoemaking were transforming many of the skilled and semi-skilled trades in the United States. The value of manufactures quadrupled during the first half of the century, and industry's share of total US commodity output doubled. But, whereas Lynn was a single-industry town, a diversity of manufacturing was typical in Philadelphia, New York, and other industrial cities of the Northeast. In these cities in 1860, shoes were still being assembled by artisans in small neighborhood shops, by domestic outworkers at home, or by workers in small-scale, nonmechanized manufactories. Yet the trend in manufacturing was definitely toward larger-scaled production. As Sean Wilentz has noted, "metropolitan industrialization," that is, a reorganization in the social relations of production, was taking place in tandem with the transformation of wage labor into a market commodity. These changes challenged workers' fundamental assumptions about work and workshop relations. All through the antebellum years, urban workers continued to assert the values identified with the notion of "the Trade," a concept steeped in the Revolutionary ideals of independence, virtue, equality, and a just republic.

Figure 3.4 The Norris Locomotive Works in Philadelphia in 1855. From *Railroad History*, no. 150 (Spring 1984): 29. Smithsonian collection (negative#77-14568). Original publication unknown.

Figure 3.5 A section of the forge shop at the Norris Locomotive Works, Philadelphia, 1855. From *United States Magazine of Science, Art, Manufacture, Agriculture, Commerce and Trade* 2 (October 1855): 158.

Industrialization spread beyond the older mercantile cities and one-industry towns of the East Coast and across the United States during the middle decades of the nineteenth century. Despite having begun to industrialize later than the eastern centers, inland cities and towns such as Cincinnati, Ohio, experienced a growth in manufacturing that followed a similar trajectory. For example, during the "Age of the Artisan" (1788–1843) Cincinnati's small, unmechanized shops produced goods according to craft traditions. However, starting in the late 1820s, expanding markets and the rise of such "new" industries as iron founding and meat packing produced deeper economic and social divisions within the Queen City. As had happened earlier in Lynn's shoe industry, the scale of production in Cincinnati increased during the "Age of Manufacture" (1843–73) and ownership became concentrated in the hands of a few entrepreneurs in each of the city's industries. Rather than nascent masters, Cincinnati's journeymen became wage laborers. Although the overall pattern of change was similar to that in the Northeast, the timing and extent of the changes in the city's leading manufactories differed.

The modernization of Cincinnati's boot and shoe industry took place over several decades. Much as had happened in Lynn, an expansion of the market, a greater centralization of production, and a more extensive division of labor preceded the introduction of steam-powered mechanization in shoe production in Cincinnati. Whereas in 1860 shoes were manufactured either in the Queen City's traditional custom shops or in its wholesale manufactories, by the 1870s Cincinnati's shoe manufacturers were purchasing the same type of new machinery that was already being used in the eastern shoe factories. Cincinnati's furniture industry was transformed as well. The city's artisan furniture makers still continued to turn out finely made and expensive custom work in the 1850s even as a number of larger manufactories producing inexpensive, ready-made furniture for sale in distant markets began to emerge. By the early 1870s, however, production had shifted from the small shops and the manufacture of expensive furniture to mammoth factories that turned out cheaper goods. The transition from handicraft to large-scale factory production was even more rapid in the city's carriage and wagon industry. This industry's transformation began with the introduction in 1872 of inter-changeable parts in carriage production, an innovation that ena-bled the manufacture of vast numbers of ready-made carriages. In yet another Cincinnati industry, meat processing, assembly-line organization, and mass production had begun even earlier than in the other local industries. In the 1830s mass production and an intricate specialization had become standard in the slaughter-houses of America's "Porkopolis," which sold their products in national and international markets.

With a wide variety of manufactures, Newark, New Jersey, had by the time of the Lynn strike already become one of the lead-ing industrial cities in the United States. More than three-quarters of its workforce were involved in some form of manufacturing. However, by 1860 competition from the Massachusetts shoe towns had reduced employment in shoemaking, one of Newark's earliest and most successful industries, to just over 5 percent of the workforce. But other local trades, such as the manufacture of hats, jewelry, and trunks and other leather products, expanded, especially as a result of the mechanization of these crafts. Traditional skills and work rhythms were disrupted as work became separated from the household and the craft shop. In many of these trades one or two firms employed a significant proportion of the workforce. With mechanization, new production methods increased output but also enabled the hiring of cheap, unskilled, labor. The growing pace of immigration into Newark during the 1840s and 1850s, rather than an increase in the hiring of local women or children, supplied the city's employers with the neces-sary workers.

Over the course of the first half of the nineteenth century, even a city like Albany, New York, which largely remained a commercial center whose economy was tied to the growth of canals in the 1820s and of the railroads during the following decades, had become a center for manufacturing. By 1860, at the time of the Lynn strike, Albany's manufacturers ranked in value on a par with those of Chicago and Pittsburgh. Many of the diversified products manufactured in Albany – chairs and cabinets, boots and shoes, bricks, pianos, stoves, even beer – were typical in kind and in scale of the industries in the rest of country then. Although most manufacturing establishments in the Capital City were typically small scale, having fewer than ten employees each, there were ten manufacturers in Albany whose workforce numbered more than fifty employees each. Among these were three stove foundries producing some $600,000 worth of stoves and employing 500 workers, or an average of 167 workers per establishment. Four smaller foundries together produced stoves worth $200,000 and employed 132 men, or an average of 33 workers each.

The coexistence of small and larger firms also characterized the brewing and boot and shoe industries in Albany. Unlike the stove foundries, which were all powered by steam, eight of the fifteen breweries in the city still relied on manual power and the rest used steam. Yet the seven steam-powered breweries produced about two-thirds of the total product value and employed three-quarters of the industry's workforce. By 1860 Albany's more than 300 industrial establishments manufactured more than two and a half times the value of goods and employed two and a half times more persons than they had ten years earlier. Nevertheless, Albany's heyday as a manufacturing center was passing. The city failed to attract significant large-scale industry, and by 1880 the growth of manufacturing in Chicago, Pittsburgh, and other cities had far outstripped that of Albany.

Textile manufacture, an industry already rooted in mass production and mechanization, experienced the growth, beginning in the 1830s, of even larger mills, ones that dwarfed those operating in Lowell, Massachusetts. Industrial expansion led to greater competition, and textile manufacturers responded by introducing labor-control techniques intended to reduce costs by increasing the productivity of mill workers. These practices included the stretch-out (owners increased the number of machines for which a worker was responsible), the speedup (foremen ran the machines at a faster pace), and the premium system (supervisors whose workers were most productive received substantial cash rewards). As one example, textile weavers in the early 1840s found themselves tending four looms that ran at almost the same speed as the two looms they had been operating before. Emulating other workers in the industrial cities of the Northeast, the "mill girls" fought back. To resist what they perceived to be a degradation of their work, workingwomen in Lowell organized the Lowell Female Labor Reform Association (LFLRA) in the mid-1840s. Allied with workingmen, these women joined a renewed political effort to pressure the Massachusetts legislature into passing laws limiting the workday to ten hours.

For labor and middle-class radicals such as Robert Dale Owen, Thomas Skidmore, Albert Brisbane, Horace Greeley, and George Henry Evans, however, "a mere shortening of hours of labor" was inadequate to the forging of the new social order that they desired. Often allied with trade unionists, these social thinkers and activists inspired a broad national reform movement in the 1840s based on the conviction that the workingman could abolish the new forms of slavery and oppression represented by mechanization only by ensuring that he could control the forces of production. The remedy for the ills of industrial society would be found in land reform, producers' cooperatives, and the founding of independent utopian communities.

The changing immigrant composition of the workforce during the middle decades of the nineteenth century added another volatile dynamic to evolving industrial relations in America. Although immigrants from Germany, Ireland, and Great Britain had been coming to America in considerable numbers since early in the century, the pace dramatically increased in the late 1840s. The Yankee farm girls who had made up the early textile workforce began leaving the mills for good by then, their places taken by French Canadian and Irish mill hands. In New York City in 1855, three-quarters of the workers in the consumer goods and building trades, such as glassworkers, shoemakers, and stonecutters and polishers, were immigrants, nearly half of them Irish. Overall, by 1870 one-third of the nation's industrial workers were immigrants. Solidarities within immigrant groups both contributed to and undermined the economic and social ties forged in the workplace.

The midcentury witnessed an upsurge in trade union growth and labor activity in the United States. At its peak, in 1853–54, more than 400 union-led strikes were recorded in New York, Pennsylvania, and other sizable American states. Organized initially into local unions, workers in the fifties then joined together to form national federations. The expansion of trade unions was severely disrupted by the economic depression that followed the panic of 1857 as well as by the labor needs of the Civil War. Yet business and industry in the North soon recovered. By the end of 1864, the number of trade unions had more than tripled and union membership was estimated to be more than 200,000. Rising prices and the growing power of their employers led the revived trade unions to focus not only on improving members' wages and working conditions but also on promoting political and economic reforms intended to remake capitalist economic relations of production.

William Sylvis, a Philadelphia iron molder who helped found the National Union of Ironmolders in 1859 and became the union's president in 1863, stands out among the labor leaders of the middle decades of the nineteenth century. In 1868 Sylvis was chosen to lead the National Labor Union, whose annual congresses brought together labor reformers and the representatives of local and national trade unions. Believing that workers needed to be organized at the ballot box as well as in the workplace, Sylvis focused on labor reform campaigns during this period that sought to mandate eight hours as the legal workday and to reshape the nation's monetary system by making greenbacks the exclusive US currency. He also attempted to establish union-owned foundries and producer cooperatives. After Sylvis's death in 1869, a militant trade union and labor reform movement continued to grow until it foundered in the economic depression that occurred in the wake of the panic of 1873.

Labor Reform and the Remaking of American Society

In 1843, as the US economy rebounded from its latest economic depression, the Fall River Mechanics' Association of Fall River, Massachusetts, called for a convention of mechanics throughout New England to consider strategies for securing the ten-hour workday. This call led to a meeting in Boston of "all those interested in the elevation of the producing classes and Industrial Reform." Convening on October 16, 1844, workers from across New England joined middle-class reformers, including land reformers from New York led by George Henry Evans of the National Reform Association and a dozen representatives of the Brook Farm utopian community, in organizing the New England Workingmen's Association (NEWA). Insisting that "the time now devoted to manual labor is unreasonable and unjust," the NEWA urged state legislators to pass a law that would prohibit corporations from requiring any employee to work more than ten hours per day. After an intense debate, the convention resolved to avoid partisan politics. Instead, broad-based labor reform associations would conduct petition drives. Another resolution, one that appealed particularly to the Brook Farm Associationists (American followers of the French social theorist Charles Fourier), endorsed the idea of "attractive industry," a system "in which every laborer [would have] a direct personal interest in the fruits of his labor."

Although both workers and reformers generally supported more immediate actions as well as reforms that called for broad social change, they parted ways on which approach should be prioritized. This conflict led to the NEWA's demise just a few years after its founding.

Workers in the 1840s were drawn in by the glowing promises of Associationists to remake society through the formation of independent utopian communities. In 1841 a group of New England Transcendentalists established Brook Farm, not far from Boston, where they hoped to demonstrate that manual and intellectual labor could coexist harmoniously. Over the next ten years more than forty Fourierist "phalanxes" or cooperative communities were established in localities across America from Massachusetts to Iowa. They attracted all classes in society, especially craft workers. Although most were abandoned not long after their founding, Brook Farm lasted six years, and the North American Phalanx, established near Red Bank, New Jersey, flourished for thirteen years. In a letter to her father, Mary Paul, one of the "associates" of the North American Phalanx, observed that, whereas in contemporary society men often were paid double what women received for doing the same work, such discrimination was impossible among Associationists because "*All* work there, and all are paid alike. Both men and women have the *same pay* for the *same* work."

Associationists assumed that the promise of industrial America could be fulfilled only by establishing communities that restructured the relations of work and that made work more pleasant and worthwhile. For George Henry Evans, a leader in the workingmen's movements of the Jacksonian era, the solution to the problems facing the producing classes lay in restoring to them their natural right to own land. The land monopoly was the "cause of the greatest evils," Evans proclaimed. "If man has a right on the earth, he has a right to land enough to raise a habitation. If he has a *right to live*, he has a right to land enough to till for his subsistence." Evans advocated that public lands be distributed in equal farm lots of 160 acres to any American who entered a claim. To force Congress to agree to open up access to free public land, Evans formed the National Reform Association in 1845. He also revived the *Working Man's Advocate* (a labor journal he had published in the 1830s) in that year, and he and his followers plastered the cities across the United States with handbills that asked workers, "Are you tired of slavery, of drudging for others – of poverty and its attendant miseries? Then Vote Yourself a Farm." There was hardly a major labor meeting during these years that Evans did not attend to promote his land reform plan.

In the years leading up to the Civil War the "land question" became a major political issue. For many Northerners, keeping the lands of the western United States open to free labor – keeping them "free soil" – was the basis of their growing opposition to slavery. Workers throughout the nation, even in the South, organized ward clubs and signed pledges to vote only for those candidates for legislative office who agreed in writing to support access to free public lands for the exclusive use of settlers. Land reform became the law in 1862 when Congress passed the Homestead Act, which gave any adult citizen or permanent immigrant the right to claim 160 acres of public land for a $10 fee, final title to be granted after five years of residence.

Like the other movements to remake industrial society, cooperative production appealed to workers in the 1840s as a means of preserving their status as skilled and independent craftsmen. The year following a failed strike in 1847, twenty iron molders in Cincinnati organized the Journeymen Moulders' Union Foundry. With a small amount of capital that they raised among themselves, the molders purchased a piece of land on the Ohio River. Friends of the cooperative foundry constructed the necessary buildings, and the foundry members elected a board of directors, a foreman, and a business agent. After the union foundry opened in August 1848, its members reinvested their profits in the business and by

January 1850 they had more than doubled the capital stock and the number of journeymen they employed. But a severe economic downturn the following year, along with underselling by local stove manufacturers, led to the cooperative venture's demise. Similar attempts in these years to become "their own employers" and to "divide the profits of their labors among themselves" were made by iron molders in other Midwestern cities, as well as by tailors, printers, and other workers in Boston, New York City, and elsewhere. None of these ventures, however, brought the hoped-for solution to the problem of workers' declining status or of the deterioration of their working conditions.

Despite the "Workingmen's" in its name, women had been active in the NEWA from the beginning. At a meeting of the NEWA in Lowell in March 1845 a constitution for the new association was adopted that specifically provided for the admission of female groups on an equal basis with male members. One of these groups was the Lowell Female Labor Reform Association (LFLRA), which had been founded in December 1844. Led by Sarah Bagley, a mill weaver since 1836, the LFLRA spearheaded petition drives in 1843 and 1844 calling on the Massachusetts legislature to enact a ten-hour workday law for the state's incorporated businesses. Referred to as the first woman labor leader in American history, Bagley, speaking before the assembled delegates at the NEWA's 1845 convention in Boston, sought to reassure the predominantly male audience that activist women did not threaten the men's sphere: "We do not expect to enter the field as soldiers in this great warfare; but we would, like the heroines of the Revolution, be permitted to furnish the soldiers with a blanket or replenish their knapsacks from our pantries." Yet Bagley never temporized on the demand for ten hours for women workers. Peaking in 1846, the LFLRA's petition drives secured more than 4,000 signatures that year.

In response to an LFLRA petition campaign in 1845, the Massachusetts House of Representatives Committee on Manufacturing appointed a committee to investigate the ten-hour issue.

Chairing the committee was William Schouler, a representative from Lowell who usually spoke on behalf of textile corporation interests. Likely expecting that "virtuous" women would be unwilling to testify, Schouler wrote to petition drive leaders Bagley and J. Q. A. Thayer that, because most of the petitioners "are female; it will be necessary for them to make the defence, or we shall be under the necessity of laying [the ten-hour issue] aside." Bagley quickly disabused Schouler of his hope to quash the women's effort before the hearings began by responding that the women stood ready to testify. The six women whom Schouler chose (each was a petition signer) all argued for the ten-hour workday. They complained about their fourteen-hour workdays, which began at 5:00 am and extended until 7:00 pm, with only short breaks for rushed meals, and about their low wages, the close quarters, the impure air from smoky whale oil lamps and the ever-present cotton dust, and the other harsh working conditions that they encountered in the mills.

Nevertheless, after visiting the mills and interviewing the owners' representatives, the investigative committee concluded that mill workers in Massachusetts enjoyed conditions that were superior to those in Great Britain and that the health of the operatives was as good as that of the general population. Whatever abuses may exist, they insisted, "The remedy is not with us." Hours could not be regulated without materially affecting wages, and "experience has taught us [that wages] can be much better regulated by the parties themselves than by the Legislature," especially because, unlike in foreign countries, "Here labor is on an equality with capital, and indeed controls it." Angered by the rebuff, the LFLRA targeted Schouler for retribution, successfully opposing his bid for re-election in the fall and thereby "consigning him to the obscurity he so justly deserves."

In rejecting the LFLRA's ten-hour petition, the legislature in Massachusetts in 1845 restated conventional economic wisdom, the assumption that government intervention violated the freedom of contract between employers and employees. Yet, just a few years before, Lemuel Shaw, the chief justice of the Supreme Judicial Court of Massachusetts, had rendered a decision in *Commonwealth v. Hunt* (1842) that questioned this assumption. *Commonwealth* involved the prosecution of the Boston Society of Journeymen Bootmakers, a union, as a criminal conspiracy. Originating in eighteenth-century England, the doctrine of criminal conspiracy had been successfully applied in the United States as early as 1806 to a trade union formed among Philadelphia's boot makers and shoemakers (*Commonwealth v. Pullis*). In 1840 Jeremiah Horne, a member of the bootmakers' society, challenged the union's right to fine him for violating its rules. After the Boston society persuaded his employer to discharge him, Horne initiated a lawsuit that charged the union with criminal conspiracy.

Despite testimony from Horne's employer that he had willingly complied with the union's request that he dismiss Horne, the trial judge, Peter Oxenbridge Thatcher, instructed the jury that the Boston society represented "a new power in the state, unknown to its constitution and laws, and subversive of their equal spirit." Apparently agreeing with Thatcher, the jury brought back a guilty verdict. Robert Rantoul, Jr., the society's lawyer, filed a bill of exceptions to Thatcher's jury instructions, and the case came before Chief Justice Shaw, a conservative judge not known for his sympathy for unions. Yet Shaw ruled in favor of the Journeymen Bootmakers. He argued that, for the concerted action of a "combination of two or more persons" to be a conspiracy, it must seek either to accomplish "some criminal or unlawful *purposes*" or to engage in an act that is not itself criminal but is accomplished by "criminal or unlawful *means.*" The indictment, "stripped ... of the qualifying epithets," Shaw asserted, came down to whether persons "engaged in the same occupation" had formed an association that they joined of their own free will and in pursuit of their own interests. His ruling acknowledged not only workers' right to organize but also their right to withhold their labor, or to strike, as long as they did so peaceably and were not in violation of existing contracts. Shaw was, in effect, extending to a union organization the same right of association that already applied to businesspeople. Given the many successful prosecutions that had followed in the wake of *Commonwealth v. Pullis*, Shaw's ruling was a landmark decision. However, criminal conspiracy prosecutions would again flourish at the end of the nineteenth century, especially through the broad application of injunctions against strikes and other union activities.

Despite the Massachusetts legislature's unwillingness to act, the NEWA and Sarah Bagley continued to press for ten-hour reform. One of the resolutions enthusiastically passed at the 1845 NEWA meeting in Lowell called for the association to publish its own newspaper, and shortly afterward the *Voice of Industry* (*VOI*) became the organization's official journal. William F. Young, the secretary of a local workingmen's association and an officer in the NEWA, was chosen to be the editor of the *VOI*, and Sarah Bagley was selected to edit the paper's "Female Department," which featured articles about women workers. Bagley announced that "Our department devoted to woman's thought will also defend woman's rights, and while it contends for physical improvement, it will not forget that she is a social, moral, and religious being." The link Bagley identified between the material and spiritual was very much in accord with Young's own "practical Christianity." Outspoken against New England's "'false and anti-republican' factory system and its 'Monied Despotism,'" Young indicted the prevailing economic order for denying producers the fruits of their toil and thereby frustrating the "great design of Creation."

A major force in the ten-hour movement, Bagley was also drawn to other contemporary movements that sought to remake American industrial society. Appearing on a NEWA platform in

1845 alongside Albert Brisbane, the leading Fourierist in America, Bagley praised the Associationists as heroes of labor's coming "revolution." A year later, Bagley and Huldah Stone, a fellow officer in the LFLRA, organized the Lowell Union of Associationists (LUA). Although not everyone who joined the LUA was a mill operative, thirty-one of the sixty-one members in the first year were women. In 1846 both Bagley and Stone attended the American Union of Associationists convention in Boston, and Stone accompanied Brisbane on his lecture tour on Fourierism. The Lowell Union also embraced consumer cooperation, and Lowell became a center of the movement, with eight successful cooperative stores in the late 1840s. Yet, as more women workers in these years left Lowell, the LUA faded. In 1847 Bagley took a job as a supervisor in the telegraph office in Lowell. The same year, she withdrew from the LFLRA, and little is known about her subsequent life.

By the late 1840s the Lowell industrial experiment had ended. The cumulative impact of increased production and an intensi-fied work pace in the textile industry made mill work less desir-able for many rural Yankee women. At the same time, a rapid increase in immigration after 1845, in particular from Ireland, transformed the ethnic makeup of the textile mill workforce. Looking at the records of the Hamilton Company's Lowell mills, Thomas Dublin found that the number of identifiable native-born women working there declined by more than 25 percent in the 1840s and then by almost 40 percent during the following dec-ade. During these years, immigrant children, as well as men and women, began to work in the mills in larger numbers. As a result, the number of foreign-born workers employed by Hamilton, which had been only 3.7 percent of the workforce in 1837, rose to 38.6 percent in 1850 and to 61.8 percent a decade later. During the 1860s and 1870s, French Canadians followed the Irish into the Lowell mills, as did Greeks, Poles, and other nationalities later in the century.

Immigrant Workers Confront Nativism

Lowell's experience with immigration was hardly unusual. Before the mid-1850s immigrants had begun streaming into cities in the United States in ever-larger numbers. Between 1845 and 1855 more than three million immigrants came to the United States, principally from Ireland and Germany. Whereas in the 1830s nearly 600,000 immigrants entered the United States, that number almost doubled in the forties and then increased again by 50 percent in the fifties. Usually drawn from the middling strata of urban artisans and rural small producers, the German skilled workers tended to be receptive to reform politics and trade unionism. Unlike the Germans, the Irish, who were heavily Catholic and overwhelmingly from rural areas, were more likely to find employment as day laborers. By 1860 almost 50 percent of the residents of New York City, Pittsburgh, and Chicago were foreign born. In Philadelphia, foreign-born residents accounted for just under 30 percent of the population, whereas in St. Louis their numbers reached almost 60 percent. As immigrants became a majority of the skilled workers in many large cities, native-born Americans frequently abandoned these trades for white-collar mercantile and professional jobs.

Beginning in the 1840s, many native-born workers responded to the growing numbers of immigrants with fear and hostility. American workers often protested that the immigrant came to this country willing to "work for fourteen and sixteen hours per day for what capital sees fit to give him." In the Massachusetts textile town of Fall River, in the 1840s the labor newspaper *The Mechanic* demanded that workers who were rebuilding the town after a devastating fire be employed for a ten-hour day. American workers stood behind the ten-hour standard and condemned the "all day men" among the Irish immigrant and rural workers for acting as the virtual slaves of the employers. In the 1840s nativism would become a potent force in politics in Philadelphia, New York, and other cities in the United States.

Kensington, a manufacturing suburb of Philadelphia, experienced bloody anti-immigrant riots in May and July 1844 as native-born Americans attacked the homes and Roman Catholic churches of Irish Americans. Almost 90 percent of Kensington's adult labor force was classified as working in manufacturing and trades, especially weaving, shoemaking, and ship building. Most of the area's workmen were native Pennsylvanians and Protestant, but in weaving more than three-quarters of the masters and workmen were of Irish birth and predominately Roman Catholic. Weaving, of both cotton and woolen cloth, was Kensington's main industry. Although Philadelphia's boosters claimed that their city had more weaving factories than any other city in the world, the trade was mainly a cottage industry, based on the putting-out system and the use of handlooms. Especially during periods of economic depression, such as the country was experiencing during the late 1830s and early 1840s, masters looked to reduce the piece rates they paid to weavers, which produced violent economic conflict. In his study of the Kensington riots of 1844, the historian David Montgomery notes that, beginning in August 1842, Kensington weavers refused to work at the fall scale offered by their employers. An agreement between the weavers and masters came in November but only after three military companies had been sent into Kensington to prevent further violence between the strikers and scabs. Nevertheless, conflict between Catholics and Protestants in Philadelphia persisted even after the economy began to improve.

Antagonism based on ethnicity and religion, paradoxically, both encouraged the formation of cross-class alliances and fragmented working-class solidarity. Since the 1780s, the coming of Irish Catholic textile workers to Philadelphia had aroused the antipathy of American- and Irish-born Protestants. In the early 1840s anti-Catholic agitation increased. Protestant leaders and congregants considered the teaching of the Bible to be the greatest safeguard America had against the evils that would "tear up every social institution by the roots, and leave nothing behind but disorder, waste, and ruin." For these Protestants the only version of the Bible that was acceptable for use in the public schools was the King James Version. Seeking to protect his Catholic congregants from a heretical book, Bishop Francis Patrick Kenrick of Philadelphia successfully lobbied the Board of Controllers to permit children whose parents were "conscientiously opposed" to be excused during Bible readings. In response, the American Republican Party, a political movement that sought, among its anti-immigrant goals, to defend the teaching of the King James Bible in the schools, took up the cause. Also in support, ninety-four leading Philadelphia clergymen pledged to strengthen Protestant education and to "awaken" the community to the dangers posed by "Romanism." They were joined in this crusade by the city's Protestant churches, Bible societies, temperance societies, and missionary agencies. Overnight, the American Republican Party, whose ranks included Protestant workers as well as a middle-class leadership of prominent local professional men and small entrepreneurs, became a political force in Philadelphia.

As tensions mounted, Bishop Kenrick sought to allay Protestant fears in the city. But, in February 1844, Hugh Clark, a Catholic school director and boss weaver from Kensington, authorized a teacher to suspend Bible reading until the school board resolved the issue. At public rallies that were attended by Catholic hecklers, American Republicans demanded Clark's resignation. In May the party attempted to hold an open-air meeting in the district only to have the speaker driven from the platform by angry Catholic weavers. At a protest a few days later a tirade against "Popery" led to a barrage of rocks and rotten vegetables. Matters turned more violent when a burst of musket fire aroused a nativist crowd to descend on Kensington's Hibernia Hose firehouse and the nearby weavers' cottages. The action ended with one nativist fatally shot and several more wounded. Nativist mobs retaliated over the next few days. Almost 3,000 troops, including citizen posses, city police, and militia from other cities, were called out to restore order, but not before thirty buildings, including Hugh Clark's home, had been burned down. In early July, after eight weeks of relative calm, a nativist crowd armed with a cannon forced the militia guarding a local Catholic church to surrender the building. Nativist mobs continued to riot and battle with the militia, resulting in more than a dozen rioters and militiamen dead and many more wounded. The riots finally came to an end as thousands of state militia troops patrolled the streets.

The American Republicans solidified their political power in Philadelphia in local elections the following February. Their total share of the vote in wards that had once been solidly Democratic reached more than 70 percent. Even in Kensington, in the districts where most of the fighting had taken place, nativists produced a victory that the press termed a "Waterloo sweep." Although the Whig Party regained political control in Philadelphia a year later, the American Republicans retained power in Kensington throughout the 1840s.

During the 1830s, Kensington's Catholic weavers had enjoyed the support of all groups of workmen in Philadelphia. Protestant and Catholic, native born and immigrant, and skilled craftsmen and factory operatives had all joined together in the General Trades' Union, a coalition of more than fifty organized trade societies that coordinated a militant labor movement in the city during this decade. But, as exemplified in the nativist riots over the teaching of the King James Bible, class solidarity among workers of all backgrounds would dissipate in the early 1840s in the face of cross-class appeals based on ethnic and religious differences. Religious affiliation proved to be a powerful force that united Protestant workingmen and Catholic workingmen separately under middle-class spiritual and political leadership. The growing political power of nativism was also felt. For example, in New York City, Protestants and Catholics battled each other during the 1840s over financial aid to the public schools and, in the spring 1844 elections, the nativist American Republican Party ticket carried most of the city's wards. Yet, in Philadelphia, New York, and elsewhere in the United States, even in the years when nativism was a compelling ideological force, class conflict did not disappear.

The nativist riots in Philadelphia and New York led to the founding in 1845 of a fraternal society, the Order of United American Mechanics (OUAM), in these cities. The OUAM was an example of class solidarity expressed on behalf of a nativist agenda. Particularly strong in artisan neighborhoods, the OUAM, in addition to excluding immigrants, barred merchants, bankers, and professionals and restricted its membership to "producers." Yet dramatic examples of interethnic class solidarity can also be found. A violent strike in 1850 by tailors in New York City united German, Irish, and native workers, and in the mid-fifties John Commerford, a leading New York radical, warned a crowd of protesting workers about the schemes of the upper class to keep them apart: "They wish to separate the American mechanics from the German, and the German from the Irish; they want to keep you in a divided condition so that you cannot concentrate your action for the benefit of yourselves and fellow workingmen." Despite such appeals, nativist anti-Catholic workers joined with middle-class antislavery and temperance groups during the 1850s to found the American, or Know-Nothing, Party, which called for reserving political office for native-born Americans and for resisting the "aggressions of the Catholic Church."

Black Workers in a White World

From the late seventeenth century to the end of the Civil War, slavery remained an almost universal experience for African Americans in the United States. Whereas in 1790 most slaves lived and worked on plantations producing tobacco in the Chesapeake area of Virginia and Maryland or rice or indigo in

South Carolina, by 1830 cotton was king in the South. By the beginning of the Civil War, the center of the slave population could be found in the states along the Mississippi River, a "black belt" of fertile, cotton-growing land that stretched from Mississippi to Georgia. Even though only 10 percent of slaveholding families owned twenty or more slaves, the large plantations set the tone for Southern society. As the self-liberated slave and outspoken abolitionist Frederick Douglass characterized the plantation, it was "a little nation itself, with its own language, its own rules, regulations, and customs." The majority of slaves, particularly the men, worked as field hands, picking cotton or harvesting sugar cane, and a small percentage of the female slaves worked in the "Big House" as domestic servants, carrying out the tasks of cooking, laundering, cleaning, and caring for the master's children. On large plantations a few male slaves worked in or around the master's house as butlers, gardeners, or coachmen.

In the areas of the South where large plantations predominated, slaves also worked as craftsmen. Large-scale planters encouraged artisanship among their slaves. Rather than depend on outside labor, a planter preferred to have the necessary shoemaking, saddle making, blacksmithing, tool repair, and other craftwork done more cheaply in a shop on the plantation. At times, a small farmer would hire a slave artisan from his planter neighbors to do his blacksmithing, shoemaking, or carpentry. A slave with artisan skills could be worth three times as much as a field hand.

In the coastline cities of the antebellum South in the 1850s many African American men, whether slave or free, worked as artisans and craftsmen, stevedores and draymen, common laborers, or barbers. Most of the slaves were hired (the wages went to their masters) to work either as domestic servants or as service tradesmen. Only about a third of all urban slaves worked in Southern industries. Many owners of slave craftsmen in these cities allowed their slaves to be their own employers or to work in their own time in return for an agreed-on weekly payment to the master. In the mid-1830s Hugh Auld apprenticed his twenty-year-old slave Frederick Bailey (who would assume the surname Douglass after fleeing to the North) to become a journeyman caulker in a shipyard in Baltimore. During the busy season, Douglass was able to earn $9 a week, which he turned over to his master, who gave him a small allowance to pay for incidentals. Shortly after he started his apprenticeship, Douglass petitioned Auld to be permitted to find his own employment and to make his own bargains for work. For being allowed such freedom Douglass was obliged to pay Auld $3 a week, whether or not he found work, and to board and clothe himself and to buy his own caulking tools.

In his *Narrative of the Life of Frederick Douglass: An American Slave, Written by Himself*, Douglass describes his experience as an apprentice ship caulker. He was at the "beck and call" of the shipyard's seventy-five carpenters, "Their word was my law. ... It was – 'Fred., come help me cant this timber here,' –'Fred., bring that roller here.' – 'Fred., go get a fresh can of water,'" and "'Halloo, nigger! Come, turn this grindstone.'" At the time, he noted that white carpenters worked side by side with black carpenters, many of whom were freemen, and that "no one seemed to see any impropriety in it." But then, "all at once," the white carpenters went on strike, announcing that they would no longer work with "free colored workmen." Convinced that their "trade" would soon fall into the hands of the free black craftsmen, they demanded that the black artisans be removed. The white apprentices in the shipyard then followed suit, protesting being forced to work with Douglass, whom they brutally attacked.

Yet, as the historian Seth Rockman notes in his study of labor in early Baltimore, during the early nineteenth century Lyndia Holiday, a thirty-year-old slave who worked as a domestic, was more typical of the urban African American workforce than was Douglass. Although some enslaved women toiled in bakeries and tobacco manufactories, by 1830 the majority lived in residential areas and, as stated in the ads, did "the housework of a small family" or did the cleaning and cooking in the taverns and inns of Southern cities. Many enslaved domestics were hired for set periods by families of modest means rather than owned by them outright. Ads appeared in the local newspapers seeking "a colored Woman, or the time of one," and offering to buy or to rent the enslaved woman from her owner for "a liberal price or wages." By the 1820s, even many of the growing number of free black women in Baltimore resided in the households of their white employers. Free black women also dominated the laundry business in the city. Although it was backbreaking labor, working as a laundress enabled an African American woman to remain at home and to avoid direct white supervision. Although most of the domestic workforce was female, prosperous households did hire or rent black men, free or slave, to serve as valets, waiters, drivers, and hostlers.

Even as cotton remained king in the antebellum Southern economy, some investors sought to diversify. One of the more profitable of these ventures was the Tredegar Iron Works in Richmond, Virginia. Preferring to employ bondsmen rather than wage laborers, Joseph Reid Anderson, the proprietor of the Tredegar Company, claimed, "It has always been considered an object of primary importance in our Country to introduce slave labour generally in the several branches of Iron manufacture." In 1842 Anderson announced that only those white workers who signed a five-year agreement to train slaves would not be discharged. At the end of this agreement in 1847, white ironworkers in the mill, correctly fearing that these slaves would be used as cheap replacements for them, went out on strike, pledging themselves "not to work, unless the negroes be removed from the Puddling Furnace, at the new mill." Anderson's response was "You have *discharged yourselves*." Making an argument on behalf of "Capital" worthy of any Northern factory owner, he lectured the white puddlers that "those who enter into his [a manufacturer's] employment must not expect to prescribe to him who he shall be at liberty to employ." The strikers were prosecuted for engaging in a "conspiracy" against their employer. Within three years of the end of the unsuccessful strike by white ironworkers, Tredegar had taken on 100 slaves, who worked alongside the 150 white iron-workers he employed. And, in the decades leading up to the Civil War, white craftsmen would repeatedly protest being forced into competition with skilled slave artisans.

After Douglass's beating at the hands of the white appren-tices, his master found him work in another Baltimore shipyard. It was at this time that Douglass resolved to finally make his escape. With the moral and material support of his wife, Anna, on the third day in September 1838, he "left my chains" and suc-ceeded in making his way by boat to New York City. After a brief stay there, Douglass continued on to New Bedford, Massachusetts, where he believed he would be able to find work as a caulker. Yet when he went to the docks in New Bedford he was told "that every white man would leave the ship ... unfinished ... if I struck a blow at my trade upon her." Instead, Douglass found work as a day laborer, sawing wood, shoveling coal, loading and unloading vessels. Such work was irregular at best. Desperately poor, his wife pregnant with their first child, Douglass appealed to his ben-efactors among the Quaker merchants. With their help, he was able to find a steadier job in the local whale oil refinery. Douglass expressed a certain pride in the respect accorded him by the white workers at the refinery: "I soon made myself useful, and, I think liked by the [white] men who worked with me."

Douglass was hardly alone among the many slaves who escaped and found at least relative freedom in the North. But Northern cities in the decades before the Civil War experienced an influx not only of escaping slaves but also of unskilled, rural-born whites. To this mix was added the unskilled Irish immigrants who emigrated to America in these years. The animus shared by the unskilled native-born white laborers and their Irish counterparts toward African American workers tended to mitigate the nativism of the antebellum period. The conflict between African American workers and Irish workers is usually explained by historians in terms of competition for the jobs at the bottom of the occupational ladder. Such tensions were often exacerbated by employers who expressed a preference for hiring "docile Negroes" over the "rowdy Irish." Yet, as the historian David Roediger has noted in his groundbreaking work *The Wages of Whiteness: Race and the Making of the American Working Class*, the Irish had far more competition for jobs from German Americans than from African Americans. Roediger explains that the concentration by the Irish on African Americans as rivals for their jobs represented an appeal to a shared race consciousness of "whiteness," that is, it reflects a conscious attempt by the Irish to distinguish themselves from the "blacks" and to be accepted by native-born workers as "white."

Denied access to "white" unions, African American workers formed benefit associations of their own for mutual protection. These groups included both the Humane Mechanics and the Coachmen's Benevolent Society, which were organized in Philadelphia in the 1820s, and the Stewards' and Cooks' Marine Benevolent Society, which was established in New York during the following decade. In July 1850 the American League of Colored Laborers was founded with Frederick Douglass as its vice president. It had been intended that the league would promote unity among mechanics in addition to fostering members' training in the agricultural and industrial arts. In fact, the society appears to have been focused more on industrial education than on becoming a trade union. Twenty years after Douglass fled the city, an African American union, the Association of Black Caulkers (ABC), was organized in Baltimore in the face of united action by German and Irish immigrants to drive black workers from the caulking trade. The white caulkers had petitioned to have the black caulkers dismissed. When these petitions failed to achieve their purpose, the whites rioted against the black caulkers. The black caulkers responded by forming the ABC in the summer of 1858. The white caulkers in turn formed their own society. Even though a local court ordered both associations to end their hostilities, the violent confrontations between black caulkers and white caulkers in Baltimore continued.

Trade Unions on the Move in the 1850s

Looking at the reaction of American society to the advance of industrialization, Norman Ware, in *The Industrial Worker, 1840–1860: The Reaction of American Industrial Society to the Advance of the Industrial Revolution*, characterized the labor movement of the 1840s as "defensive," as a backward-looking attempt to forestall the encroachment of industrialization by preserving the way of life that workers believed was being eroded under the new industrial order. In contrast, Ware celebrated "the labor uprising of the 1850s" as "aggressive," as a "legitimate industrial movement" based in the activities of modern trade unions that had been organized either as craft benefit societies or as protective unions. Unlike workers in the labor reform movements of the 1840s, workers in the 1850s, according to Ware, accepted the inevitability of the new industrialism and relied on the strike as their main weapon.

The binary model employed by Ware to differentiate between the labor movements of the 1840s and the 1850s, and his obvious preference for what he believed was labor's more limited and wage-conscious struggle in the latter decade, oversimplifies what happened in these decades as well as in those that followed. An overtly political labor movement did not disappear with the end of the 1840s. Unions could and frequently did embrace both political and economic approaches to improving workers' living conditions. The trade union manifestos of the 1850s and beyond, as Sean Wilentz has noted, "bristled" with attacks on "'the wages system' – and not simply inadequate wages – as the source of their [workers'] plight, a threat to their republican citizenship." This more expanded view of the role of the labor movement should also be understood as the most compelling lesson of the cordwainers' 1860 strike in Lynn.

On the evening of May 23, 1850, twenty-eight printers in Albany, New York, gathered in a local hotel to organize a union. Four days later they met again, elected officers, and adopted a constitution. A "Typographical Association" was needed, according to Myron H. Rooker, a leader of the organizing movement, in order "to stay the present downward tendency of the profession – to advance and preserve the character of the Art of Arts." In July of the same year, more than 400 printers in Philadelphia signed an agreement to unite. "The *Journeymen Printers*" of Philadelphia, they announced in their "Declaration of Principles," had joined "themselves together ... to promote our interests, advance our moral and intellectual condition and give weight and importance to our acts. ... *In union there is* strength." Like their fellow skilled craftsmen in Albany, and like printers in Boston, New York City, and elsewhere at this time, Philadelphia's printers organized a union as an agency to defend their craft traditions and to secure their economic well-being.

As one of its first actions, the union of Albany printers formed a committee to investigate the state of the printing trade in the city. What they found confirmed their anxiety. More than half of the city's printers were "two-thirders," partially trained boys who were hired as journeymen and paid two-thirds the going rate for fully trained workers. Because of what they called "an unjustified system of underbidding competition," the "honorable offices," those that maintained traditional standards, were forced to compete with "mongrel" offices. Only by formalizing traditional apprentice regulations would the "rising generation" be trained to be good workmen and thereby "maintain the dignity, honor and justice" of the trade.

Yet how could these noble goals be attained? The Albany printers rejected independent action, such as going out on strike: "We deprecate all violent measures. Our weapon must be moral suasion and combined and vigorous action by ourselves and for ourselves." Beyond organizing themselves, they rested their hopes for ameliorating their condition on "a respectful and reasonable remonstrance to the employers. ... *If they wish good to themselves, let them come up with us and help us.*" Virtually the same recommendation was made by the printers' union in New York City as part of their inquiry into the state of the trade. At their first meeting, on January 19, 1850, the New York printers elected Horace Greeley, the owner of the New York *Tribune*, as president. An "honorable" proprietor (he paid the highest wages in the trade) and a critic of the terrible hold that the "Wages system had on American society," Greeley nevertheless opposed strikes or "Battles of any kind" between employers and employees. Much as the printers in Albany did, the *Tribune*'s editor put his faith in the tenets of the free labor order, especially the idea that a harmony of interests existed in America between labor and capital.

Greeley was hardly alone in his faith in the free labor order. A society based on free labor was celebrated in the 1850s by Abraham Lincoln and by many Northerners regardless of political party. Under the free labor system of the North, class divisions would not become permanent because each laborer was assumed to have the opportunity to become independent, either as a craftsman or as a landowning farmer. Because all members of society would benefit from economic growth, a mutuality of interests was presumed to exist between the employer and the employed. In the same year that they established their union, the Albany printers joined with their employers and with leading members of the community to celebrate the independence achieved by Edward Gilbert, a former member of their ranks who had become the owner of a newspaper in California and had been elected to Congress from that state. At the public dinner honoring Gilbert, Albany's mayor pointed to Gilbert's success as "a bright example of the rewards which a combination of industry, enterprise, and integrity always commands." John Nafew, a leader of the union, also spoke in praise of Gilbert. In toasting the guest of honor, Nafew drew a connection between the former Albany printer and the quintessential American printer, Benjamin Franklin, "May his [Franklin's] success prompt some brother of the craft to emulate his fame, and gather laurels as rich as Prometheus." Events like the Gilbert dinner served as public rituals during which members of the community came together to celebrate their shared faith in the social progress made possible by the free labor order.

Not all printers were as reluctant as those in Albany and New York City to engage in militant action. The conditions in the printing industry in Philadelphia mirrored those in both of the other cities. Philadelphia's printers too deplored the hiring of "two-thirders" whose lower pay, they were certain, was driving the wages down for all the journeymen. Yet, unlike the unions in the two Empire State cities, Philadelphia's organized journeymen responded to these conditions not just by adopting a new scale of prices but also by going out on strike to enforce it. The strike began on September 2, 1850, and to ensure solidarity among the journeymen, the union formed a vigilance committee to keep a "Rat List" of the "unworthy members of the trade" that it could send to every union or printers' society in the country. To support the printers who were out on strike, the union assessed an extra fee from employed members and used that money to pay the unemployed printers to produce a new edition of Daniel Defoe's novel *Robinson Crusoe* for sale to the public. The union called off the strike on December 7, 1850, after most of the printing offices had accepted its price scale.

Despite their differences over tactics, the printers' unions in all three cities participated in the movement to organize a national typographical union. In an effort to "establish connection with each other" for united action "on every question involving the interests of the trade," printers assembled early in December 1850 in a national convention in New York City. Two years later, in 1852, delegates from twelve cities met in Cincinnati to formally launch the National Typographical Union.

The printers believed that in establishing the first national trade union in the United States they were setting an example for the "laborers of all trades" who are looking for "some sure plan of amelioration which they can all adopt." Indeed, from 1852 to just prior to the panic of 1857 ten more national unions were established. Like that of the printers, most of these new national unions were formed by workers in craft trades, such as hat finishers, plumbers, stonecutters, and cigar makers. Although only three of these unions survived the panic, five other trades organized national unions before the start of the Civil War. Unlike members of the earlier national unions, the iron molders, mule spinners, and machinists and blacksmiths were part of the factory system. In many of the new national unions, real power remained in the hands of the locals. However, the national unions of both the iron molders and the machinists and blacksmiths, following the typographers' example, developed effective administrative structures.

In the nineteenth century, iron foundries in the United States produced cast-iron goods such as stoves, kitchen utensils, hinges, and gear wheels from molten iron poured into molds. Conditions in the industry began to change as large employers, looking to dominate the growing market, attempted to exert greater control over production. The iron founders, echoing the introduction of two-thirders in printing, sought to bring into their foundries partially trained workers called "berkshires," or helpers, who would be paid by the skilled molders. The founders also tried to redefine the labor process, forcing each molder to fabricate only one stove part rather than the entire stove.

Both of these changes undercut the need for skilled molders and therefore their wages and security.

As tension in the industry mounted, strikes occurred in the early 1850s in stove-molding centers such as Albany and Troy, New York, and Philadelphia. A strike in the City of Brotherly Love led to the formation on July 16, 1855, of the Journeymen Stove and Hollow-ware Moulders' Union of Philadelphia. The union's preamble declared: "'Wealth is power.' ... In the present organization of society, labourers single handed are powerless ... but combined there is no power of wrong they may not openly defy." The union's constitution prohibited members from working below a standard weekly wage, established a strike fund, and required members to pledge that they would "procure employment for a member in preference to others."

Within four years, molders' unions had also been organized in Troy and Albany and in other cities and towns. The stove molders in both of the New York cities formed their unions in 1859 in response to "odious rules and obnoxious conditions" that the iron founders sought to impose, which included requiring molders to hire "berkshires," paying workers in "truck" or store orders, and mandating that workers sign contracts forfeiting the right to recover damages if injured on the job. The Troy molders went out on strike in March 1859 against these new conditions, and the manufacturers conceded after two and a half weeks. But in Albany the employers organized a founders' league in April 1859 and, in effect, "locked out" their workers. Members of the league agreed not to employ any union molder and to shut their works at the first sign of a union movement. For the owners the issue was not simply who determined the molders' wages. The founders were equally concerned about the workers' attempt "to introduce certain regulations" in the foundries, such as shop committees to enforce union rules, that they as "proprietors must naturally resist." Although an end to the lockout was not reported in the local newspapers, it appears that one of the city's largest foundries was running as a "union shop" by September "and that other Albany foundries quickly followed suit."

The Albany lockout inspired iron molders in locals from around the country to attend a convention in Philadelphia in July 1859 to discuss forming a national molders' union. Although they accomplished little else, the thirty-five delegates from twelve locals did agree to meet again the following year in Albany and they appointed William Sylvis, an iron molder from Philadelphia, to head a committee to issue "an address" to molders throughout the United States on the need to form a national organization. For the next ten years, Sylvis was a key figure in the development of a national iron molders' union that became a model for labor organization in general.

Sylvis's address to the iron molders offers a template for producerist thought in nineteenth-century America. Each year, "the capital of the country becomes more and more concentrated in the hands of the few," and as a result "the laboring-classes are impoverished." Will the molders of America "receive the equivalent of our labor sufficient to maintain us in comparative independence and respectability," or must they be forced "to bow the suppliant knee to wealth"? In the formation of a national union embracing every molder "lies our only hope." In 1860 the National Union of Iron Molders was formally launched and Sylvis was elected its national treasurer. His 1859 "Address to Moulders" was incorporated as the preamble to the new union's constitution.

The transformation in the relations of production in the workplace and in society that accompanied industrial expansion posed a challenge to the faith that many Americans shared in the free labor order. Although many skilled workers in the United States faced common problems during the 1840s and 1850s, they often responded to industrialization in markedly different ways. Both the printers and the molders, for example, confronted employers who sought to create a partially trained cheap labor pool. Hoping to avoid direct conflict, the printers took refuge in appeals to "honorable" employers, calling on them to reaffirm their commitment to the ideal that a harmony of interests existed between employers and employed. The molders appear not to have held any such illusions about their employers. In their readiness to do battle on the helper and apprentice issues, the molders, especially William Sylvis, were clearly prepared to directly challenge the accepted notions of the free labor order.

CHAPTER FOUR

From the Civil War to the Panic of 1873

Labor and the War

Perhaps as many as one-half of the workingmen in the North enlisted in the Union army after the firing on Fort Sumter in 1861, according to a US Senate report produced at the end of the war. Prior to the war Northern workers had responded to the sectional divisions caused by slavery much as their fellow Americans had. Strong abolitionist sentiment prevailed among New England workers whereas no great concern over the plight of the African American slave was expressed in other parts of the country. Yet most workers supported Lincoln because he promised a Homestead Act and embraced the Republican Party's platform of "Free Soil, Free Labor, Free Men." Nevertheless, a meeting of the Workingmen of Massachusetts at Faneuil Hall in Boston in December 1860 declared, "We are weary of the question of slavery; it is a matter which does not concern us." But the workers' intense nationalism and commitment to democracy quickly resolved such differences once the war began. Whole union locals entered the army to fight as a unit.

The Dawning of American Labor: The New Republic to the Industrial Age,
First Edition. Brian Greenberg.
© 2018 John Wiley & Sons, Inc. Published 2018 by John Wiley & Sons, Inc.

The loss in union members brought about by workers' rapid response to President Lincoln's call for volunteers, as well as the immediate economic disruption caused by the war, short-circuited the growing labor movement of the late 1850s. By the end of 1861 iron molders' locals were all but extinct, and the national union convention called for January 1862 did not even meet. But labor's downward turn at the outset of the war quickly dissipated, and a trade union revival was under way by mid-1862. So many unions had either regrouped or organized anew that by December 1865 there were some 300 locals in sixty-nine trades in the United States. For many workers, the Civil War heightened their sense of grievance over the developing industrial order and encouraged them to look to both trade union organization and labor reform as the necessary means to secure their rights.

Workers' wartime service in what became a fight for freedom spurred even further militancy at the end of the war. Ira Steward, a leader of the eight-hour workday movement during the 1860s, told a Boston rally of workingmen in November 1865, "We yet want it known that the workingmen of America will in future claim a more equal share in the wealth their industry creates in peace and a more equal participation in the privileges and blessing of those free institutions, defended by their manhood on many a bloody field of battle." In *Beyond Equality: Labor and the Radical Republicans, 1862–1872*, David Montgomery, the leading historian of labor in the Civil War era, calculates that by 1870 more than 300,000 workers belonged to some 1,500 trade unions. National organizations of trade unions also rebounded. These nationals, along with local unions, city trade assemblies, and labor reform organizations, met in Baltimore in August 1866 to launch the National Labor Union (NLU). At the annual NLU congresses over the next four years, delegates debated and defined the labor movement's reform agenda. Then, in 1870, the NLU split into two factions, the "industrial," which contained the

Figure 4.1   William Sylvis. In the late 1850s and 1860s William Sylvis led the organization of both the Iron Molders' International Union and the National Labor Union. From the Terence Vincent Powderly Photographic Collection. Courtesy of The American Catholic History Research Center and University Archives (ACUA), the Catholic University of America, Washington, DC.

national unions, and the "political," which would be formally organized two years later as the National Labor Reform Party. It took the depression that followed the panic of 1873 to bring to an end this wartime and post-Civil War upsurge in the nationwide labor reform movement.

After serving briefly in the Union army, William Sylvis, the Philadelphia molder who had helped organize the molders' first national union in 1859 and who later led the NLU, took charge of the iron molders' effort to rebuild their union. In January 1863 twenty-one locals gathered in Pittsburgh and elected Sylvis president of the newly renamed Iron Molders' International Union (IMIU). Soon after, he began a four-month organizing tour of iron-molding cities and towns across the United States and into Canada. Sylvis's organizing tours continued over the next few years, and by 1867 the union had reached its highest point, comprising 149 locals and more than 8,600 members. Beyond his achievements as an organizer, Sylvis, in the words of his biographer, Jonathan Grossman, led a "silent revolution" in union administration. To maintain a more militant union, he reformed its dues structure, improved its system of strike relief, tamed the locals' use of unauthorized or "wildcat" strikes, and developed a union card system and other administrative procedures. In addition, Sylvis established the *Iron Molders' Journal* as a means of giving the union a public voice.

Even as he continued to actively rebuild his union during the war, Sylvis had begun to question whether organization alone was sufficient to overcome the power of concentrated capital. "The fact is, if every working man in America was a good law-abiding member of his union we would still be subject to the whims and caprice of capitalists," he declared during a debate in 1866 with A. C. Cameron, the editor of the *Workingman's Advocate*. Sylvis had come to believe that trade unions and strikes, although necessary to resist a downward spiral in the condition of workers, still could bring the workers only "temporary relief." The fundamental cause of all workers' problems lay in "the WAGES SYSTEM." In the years following the end of the Civil War until his death in 1869, Sylvis was at the forefront of a wide-ranging labor reform movement that attracted middle-class and labor radicals committed to resisting the formation of a permanent wage-earning class in America. Seeking more enduring relief, Sylvis, Steward, Cameron, and other labor and reform activists in the immediate postbellum era espoused the formation of worker-owned producer cooperatives, the acceptance of eight hours as the working day, and the reform of the money system or "greenbackism," as well as the creation of a labor party. For them, only by adopting such reforms could

America remain a republic, a nation in which there was no distinction between the economic, social, and political rights owed each member of the community.

The Great Lockout of 1866

The effectiveness of the Iron Molders' International Union derived from the union's ability to exert control over iron molding and to enforce the closed shop. To counter the union's extensive power in their industry, employers convened a national conference in Albany in March 1866 for the purpose of forming the National Stove Manufacturers' and Iron Founders' Association. A national employers' organization was needed, they asserted, to "protect their general interests" and to resist "any and all actions of the Molders' Union" that the employers deemed interfered "with our right to control our own workshops, and to manage our own business." The formation of an employers' organization by the stove founders reflected a general trend among manufacturers in the United States away from their long-held commitment to free labor ideals. They understood the growing permanent wage-earning status or proletarianization of workers that was taking place after the Civil War as a consequence of individual failure and not, as the historian Sven Beckert has observed in *The Monied Metropolis: New York City and the Consolidation of the American Bourgeoisie, 1850–1896*, of large-scale structural social change. As a result, American industrialists began to recast their relations with those in their employ.

In the months just before the founders' conference, the local molders' union in Troy demanded that the scale of wages paid in each shop should be the same and that there should be a 25 percent increase. In addition, Troy's local declared that, by January 1, 1867, molders should be paid by the day rather than by the piece, an employee seeking work should apply to the union's shop committee rather than to the company's foreman, and the union would enforce a standard of one apprentice for every ten molders. The bosses responded by posting notices on March 16 in every foundry in Troy and Albany (whose workers had followed Troy's lead) announcing the formation of the founders' association and rejecting the molders' demands. They further resolved that it was their intention to introduce all the "apprentices or helpers we deem advisable," that they would not "allow any Union Committees in our shops," and that in every possible way they would "free our shops of all dictation or interference on the part of our employees." To Sylvis, the demands of the newly formed iron founders' and stove molders' association constituted a declaration of "war upon our organization for the simple purpose of accomplishing its destruction." Molders in both cities rallied and "swore passionately" that they would not go back to work until these "obnoxious notices" were withdrawn. The "Great Lockout of 1866" was on.

At this point Sylvis intervened. As the lockout spread to other molding centers in Kentucky, Ohio, Virginia, California, and Canada, he decided to limit the strike to the two New York molding centers and to the shops in Cincinnati because success in these three areas would, he projected, break the founders' national organization. Sylvis's strategy worked. The founders agreed to cooperate with union committees in their shops and to increase the number of apprentices only when the supply of molders was inadequate. The outcome was "a complete victory," Sylvis justifiably boasted. But, despite their defeat in the Great Lockout, the founders and stove manufactures resumed their war with the molders during the winter of 1867–68, and this time the employers came out on top.

By 1866, Sylvis had begun to question whether "combinations," that is, union organization and strikes, were in themselves sufficient means to "break down our present system of centralization, monopoly, and extortion." Even during the Civil War, when the supply of labor was diminished and demand for workers intensified – an economic state of affairs that should have enhanced their bargaining power – workers found that their wages did not keep pace with inflation, the rising prices of the articles that they purchased. "The tendency of the price of labor," Sylvis concluded, "is ever downward." Under present conditions, a few individuals "arrogate to themselves the right to the enjoyment of all power and wealth in the world, to make labor subservient to their will," to "own" and "use" it as they would "their machinery." As a result, "Co-operation" was the next great step, "the true remedy for the evils of society." Workers will be able "to secure a fair standard of wages and a fair share of the profits arising from our industry" only when they can be "a shareholder and a partner" in the enterprises in which they labor. Thus during the Great Lockout Sylvis encouraged the molders in Troy and Albany to open their own foundries.

By the end of 1866, Albany's molders had formed a cooperative foundry, the Union Foundry Association (UFA), to be owned and run by the workers. They raised a capital fund of $50,000 by selling 500 shares at $100 each. After the owner-operators elected association officers, including a superintendent, they purchased a local stove foundry and opened it for business in January 1867. At the end of the foundry's first year, the UFA declared an 80 percent dividend. The following year, a second cooperative foundry was opened in Albany. In Troy in April 1866, even before the founding of the UFA in Albany, the stove molders' union had started its own cooperative foundry. Four months later, the Troy cooperative turned its first cast. The foundry employed only twenty molders at first, but within half a year of operation the Troy cooperative was able to report that it employed seventy-five molders, all except two of whom were shareholders. Soon the union was operating three such cooperatives in Troy. The Albany and Troy cooperatives would continue in successful operation for a few years. Furthermore, by the end of 1869 the IMIU had opened fourteen cooperatives, primarily in New York and Pennsylvania.

Convinced by the success of these union-operated foundries, and certain that cooperation represented the "true remedy for the evils of society," Sylvis called on the members of the IMIU to embrace cooperation. At the 1867 IMIU convention the Committee of Cooperation resolved that it considered cooperatives "the main lever with which the workingmen of this country are to be raised to their true position that is of becoming the proprietors of what they produce." The same year, the IMIU elected five directors and established rules for operating a national union-sponsored cooperative to be opened in Pittsburgh. Capital stock in the International's cooperative was set at $50,000; shares would be sold at from $5 to $100 each, with a limit of $1,000 in stock that could be held by any one individual; and no member could have more than one vote. Hoping to establish an IMIU cooperative in every important molding center, the union added "Protective and Co-operative" to its name in 1868. Despite the high hopes for it, the IMIU's national cooperative suffered financial difficulties from the outset and, in 1870, a year after Sylvis's death, the national union's biennial convention in Philadelphia abandoned cooperation as a goal. The cooperative foundries in Albany and Troy, unable to raise sufficient capital to successfully continue their operations, had shared the fate of the IMIU foundry by the early 1870s.

Sylvis's moral vision of a regenerated America encompassed his faith in the social utility of skilled labor and his conviction that every citizen should achieve a moderate prosperity or competence. Drawing inspiration equally from the nineteenth-century small-producer tradition associated with Thomas Jefferson and from his own deeply ingrained Methodism, Sylvis had explained to the delegates at the 1865 IMIU convention in Chicago that "small capitals are productive of happiness and industry, large ones become pernicious, by giving to one great capitalist the profits of wages of hundreds and thousands of workmen." Only when laborers controlled the places in which they worked through cooperation, Sylvis was certain, would the identity of interests, impossible under the wage labor system, be achieved and justice be secured for working people.

Sylvis's republican ideas blended easily with his deep-seated religious faith. As a young man he had taught Sunday school at his Methodist church, and he remained a committed "cold-water man" throughout his life. Just as William Heighton's labor vision in the late 1820s of a just republic was bound up with his yearning to create God's true community, so too did Sylvis's annual convention addresses to assembled iron molders in the 1860s resound with rousing tributes to the moral benefit of labor reform. Sylvis's public statements resonated with the Wesleyan doctrine of free agency, "with which an all-wise Creator has endowed mankind." "Our aim," he pronounced at the 1867 convention, "is to reach that standard in society which will enable us to be recognized as free agents." Cooperative production was synonymous with "self-help," the only means by which workers could ever become free agents. Sylvis called on union members to never forget that "success depends on their own efforts. *It is not what is done for people, but what people do for themselves, that acts upon their character and condition.*" What Sylvis hoped to achieve was not individual success but the collective advance of all producers. Worker-owned enterprise would recast rather than simply ameliorate the relations of production, assuring workers of a cooperative rather than a competitive future.

"Eight Hours for Work, Eight Hours for Rest, and Eight Hours for Recreation"

By 1867 Sylvis's labor reform agenda also included, as he told the IMIU convention, making eight hours "a legal day's work." But Sylvis did not want strikes for shorter hours; rather, "what we want is agitation, education, and legislation." An economic and

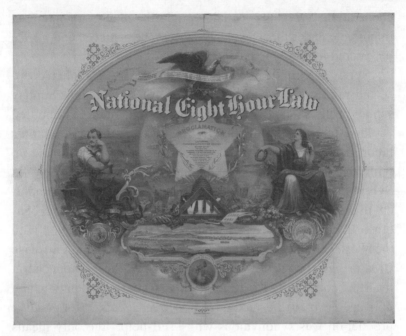

Figure 4.2   The National Eight Hour Law. Library of Congress Prints and Photographic Division, Washington, DC.

political reform movement for eight hours began right after the end of the Civil War. Closely identified with Ira Steward, a prominent leader of the Machinists' and Blacksmiths' International Union and the founder of the Boston Eight Hour League, the shorter-hours movement was in these years, as it had been in the 1830s and 1840s, as much a social and moral crusade as an economic and political campaign.

Steward and his eight-hour followers rejected the prevailing theory that an "iron law of wages," determined by the "law" of supply and demand or fixed by a market-driven wage fund created by capitalists, should prescribe what workers could earn in a free-market economy. Workers were not to be regarded as simply another cost of production. Steward insisted, instead, that limiting the workday to eight hours would provide workers with the leisure time they needed to cultivate their intellectual faculties and thereby raise their standard of living. Ultimately, as Wendell Phillips, the former abolitionist and an activist in labor reform in post-Civil War Massachusetts, observed, "the rate of wages really depends on what the workman thinks will buy him the necessities of life." Passage of an eight-hour law would "lift" American workers from "the deadening routine of mere toil."

In November 1865 Phillips told a group of Boston workers meeting in Faneuil Hall in support of the eight-hour workday that throughout his life he had opposed the idea that the "laborer must necessarily be owned by the capitalists or individuals." As the crusade against slavery was nearing its end with the close of the Civil War, "we fitly commence a struggle to define and arrange the true relations of capital and labor." The demand for the eight-hour workday was the first labor reform issue after the Civil War to develop mass support among workers. The slogan "EIGHT HOURS, A Legal Day's Work for Freemen" was emblazoned on the masthead of *Fincher's Trades Review*, an important national labor newspaper of the day. The New York State Workingmen's Assembly, organized in Albany in 1865, was committed to establishing the eight-hour standard through legislation, and the postbellum National Labor Union also endorsed the eight-hour day as part of its reform agenda. An eight-hour league organized in Albany in 1865 called on workers to unite "in a solid phalanx" behind securing an eight-hour law in order to achieve a "more just and equitable division of time and remuneration." Beyond its potential immediate benefits, an eight-hour law became for workers a symbol of a moral commitment by the community to uphold the dignity and opportunity promised to them under the free labor system.

Organized in 1864 by Steward, George McNeill, E. H. Rogers, and other labor activists, the Boston Labor Reform Association (BLRA) was dedicated to securing an eight-hour law in

Massachusetts. Reflecting Steward's ideas about the benefits to workers of an eight-hour workday, the BLRA in its first report announced that "*real comforts and proper leisure for the people* is the controlling idea of this movement." In 1865 the Massachusetts state legislature accepted a member's proposal that it consider a law to regulate the hours of labor. Viewing the issue as very complex, the House Judiciary Committee recommended the appointment of a special committee to examine the proposed legislation. This would be the first of several special committees that the Massachusetts legislature would create during the later 1860s to study the shorter-hours issue.

In early April 1865 the Joint Special Committee held a series of evening meetings to enable workingmen to testify without having to lose a day's wages. The labor newspaper the *Daily Evening Voice* (*DEV*) reported that dozens of wage workers, union leaders, and even sympathetic employers spoke out at these meetings on behalf of the physical, mental, and moral advantages of an eight-hour workday. In his testimony and other statements published at this time, Steward made an essentially consumptionist case for the eight-hour workday. The present system, he contended, did not provide workers with sufficient time for self-improvement: "The questions with employers were how many hours can I keep my machinery running? How many can the men endure?" But "[m]en who labor excessively," he insisted, "are robbed of all ambition to ask for anything more than will satisfy their bodily necessities." Increased leisure would encourage workers to "cultivate tastes and create wants in addition to mere physical comforts." Moreover, the higher economic and intellectual standard of living among workers that resulted from shorter hours would stimulate consumer spending, which would in turn create more jobs and more profits as well as a demand for higher wages to meet these new wants. The labor movement, Steward declared, was unified in support of eight hours as the crucial first step "in the elevation of the working classes."

On April 28, 1865, the Joint Special Committee presented its report to the Massachusetts House. The committee apparently agreed with the idea that the eight-hour workday would be an economic boon to the state. They speculated that shorter hours would result in a more productive workforce and would enable the state to expend fewer resources in attempting to control the social problems generated by an overworked and undereducated working population. Despite these potential advantages, the committee did not present an eight-hour bill for the current legislature to consider. Instead, they proposed that the governor appoint a commission to report to the next legislature on a possible bill.

The legislature endorsed the committee's recommendation, and in April 1865 Governor John A. Andrew appointed the Special Commission on the Hours of Labor. This commission's report, issued in February 1866, documented the distressing working conditions that existed in the state and acknowledged the overwhelming support among workers for eight-hour legislation. Although the commissioners unanimously supported legislation to ban the employment of children between the ages of ten and fourteen and to prevent youths under the age of eighteen from working more than ten hours a day, or sixty hours a week, in factories, the majority emphatically opposed passage of an eight-hour law. In this they appear to have accepted the views expressed to the special commission by manufacturers in the state. The employers testified that their employees were, like they themselves, "economic men," that is, the workers were solely concerned with making more money. For this reason they believed that their employees should be free to choose to work longer hours to increase their income. Some employers also expressed the paternalistic concern that shortening the workday would lead workers to spend their increased leisure time in "Licentiousness, gluttony, drunkenness, [and] exposure to bad habits." Pointing to himself as an example of the benefits of a longer workday, one employer testified that he had "worked 11, 12, 14, and 15 hours a day, and have as yet had no bad effects from it, but rather have been strengthened." A state-mandated eight-hour workday represented an unwarranted interference in the bargaining between an employer and employee and would subvert the individual property rights of both capital and labor.

The commissioners, echoing earlier legislative responses to reform efforts to establish a ten-hour workday, contended that a liberty of contract existed between employer and employee. Because it would "apply one measure of time to all kinds of labor" such legislation was "unsound in principle." The commission insisted that the solution to the problems that workers faced rested in their own hands: "Let the great body of working men prove by temperate and industrious habits, by ambition in work and workmanship, by the practice of economy that will help them *to become their own capitalists*, by co-operative labor, securing to each workman a share of the profits of his work." Cooperation appealed to the legislators because it did not require any state intervention in the operation of the free market.

Given the politicians' unwillingness to enact an eight-hour law, Steward and other labor reformers in Massachusetts were, by 1866, calling for workers to free themselves from the established parties and elect individuals who would represent their interests. Wendell Phillips urged workers to "go into the political field, and by the voice of forty thousand workmen say, 'We mean that eight hours shall be a day's work, and no man shall go into office who opposes it.'" The *DEV* spearheaded an effort to enlist Phillips in the cause, and in mid-September 1866 the newly formed Workingmen's Party nominated the former abolitionist for the US Congress. Believing that he could better serve "our cause" out of Congress than in it, Phillips quickly declined the nomination. Although unwilling to run for office himself, Phillips remained active in the expanding eight-hour political movement in Massachusetts.

The BLRA led a political movement in Massachusetts in the 1860s that, like the ten-hour movement twenty years earlier, assumed that deciding what constituted a legal workday was a right guaranteed to all Americans as citizen-producers. In their formulation of this right, eight-hour radicals went beyond the notion of equality that was, as Montgomery has shown in *Beyond Equality*, his seminal work on labor and the Radical Republicans during these years, acceptable to the state's political establishment. By attempting to make the determination of the number of hours in the workday an inalienable right of workers as citizens, the labor reform movement challenged the control that employers believed was guaranteed to them as property owners. They and their allies among the state's political leaders condemned any state action designed to interfere with the free labor contract.

Even though the shorter work-hours movement made little headway in Massachusetts, by 1868 eight states had enacted eight-hour laws and Congress had made eight hours the standard working day for federal government employees. In New York in 1865, at its first convention, the New York State Workingmen's Assembly called on the state's workers to promote discussion in the press and to hold public rallies in support of an eight-hour law. In Albany the city trades assembly passed a resolution asking the Albany Common Council to incorporate an eight-hour clause into all future city contracts. The eight-hour league organized by the Albany trades assembly also wrote letters to all candidates for the state legislature calling on them to endorse an eight-hour law. When a local candidate running for the State Assembly failed to respond, the league posted a notice in the area's newspapers advising local workers that he did not support their cause. The candidate quickly recanted, and the league told workers to vote as they wanted.

In 1867 New York's state legislature finally passed an eight-hour law. But the law provided no penalties for violators.

Moreover, it included a clause that preserved full "freedom of contract" rights, essentially leaving the issue to be resolved between individual employers and employees. Believing that the passage of just laws was sufficient, labor's eight-hour proponents had not contemplated the development of a bureaucratic agency to administer the new law. Instead, workers throughout New York State went out on strike and took to the streets to enforce the eight-hour statute. Among them were workers in the West Albany repair shops of the New York Central Railroad (NYCRR) who, in the spring of 1868, struck for eight hours and full pay. But a lack of support from other NYCRR train workers (engineers, brakemen, and switchmen) and from shop workers in other trades in Albany undermined the repairmen's strike, and the West Albany workers had to accept a company-offered compromise of ten hours and full wages. The unions in Albany did show labor solidarity later, however, during the summer, when they came out in force to rally in support of bricklayers in New York City who were striking for eight hours.

The strike by the bricklayers' union in New York City began in June 1868 and lasted through the summer construction season. As an inducement to employers to agree to eight hours, the bricklayers offered to accept a 10 percent reduction in their daily wages. The employers responded by forming their own association. They not only were opposed to eight hours but also sought to nullify union limits on apprentices as well as any other union work rules. For workers throughout the state, the strike in New York City became a test case for eight hours. A rally in the city on August 12 in support of the bricklayers drew thousands. Alexander Troup, a leader of the typographical union, paid tribute to the bricklayers as the advance guard of the eight-hour demand. The bricklayers' union received almost $30,000 in contributions from other unions and individuals. But the bricklayers' national union was divided over whether to support local strikes and did not aid the strikers; nor did New York's plasterers agree to engage in a sympathy walkout. As the strike dragged on, employers recruited strikebreakers from outside New York. Even though by mid-fall one city local reported that two-thirds of its members were working eight hours, in the end the strike had exhausted both parties and the issue remained unsettled. In 1869 most of New York's bricklayers appear to be again working a ten-hour day.

Two years later, nineteen of New York City's trade unions led a "large demonstration" that called for enforcement of New York's eight-hour law "which had been nominally passed, but was ... disregarded by the state government." As many as 20,000 workers, including contingents of African American plasterers and waiters and a black fife-and-drum corps, are reported to have marched carrying banners that proclaimed, "Our strength lies in the justice of our cause" and "Peaceably If We Can, Forcibly If We Must." At a mass meeting held at the Cooper Institute and chaired by William J. Jessup, president of the New York State Workingmen's Assembly, the gathering of trade unionists adopted many resolutions, including one that demanded "the abolition of class legislation by which the working classes were said to be daily cheated and robbed." The trade unionists also listened to an address from Ira Steward of the Boston Eight Hour League.

A second wave of strikes for eight hours in New York occurred in 1872 and was more successful in the short run, but this victory was quickly undone during the depression that followed the 1873 panic. Despite the repeated setbacks for the eight-hour movement in the years immediately following the end of the Civil War, trade unionists and middle-class labor reformers in Massachusetts had succeeded in establishing an active, if volatile, alliance. In 1869, having already refused to pass an eight-hour law, the state legislature also rejected a request from the Knights of St. Crispin, a recently reorganized shoemakers' union, to incorporate their planned cooperative factories and stores. Instead, the legislature agreed to create a Bureau of Labor Statistics (BLS) to provide accurate information about wages, hours, working conditions, and living standards. Formation of a labor statistics bureau had been a recommendation made by the earlier special commissions on the hours of labor and had been lobbied for by the state's labor reformers throughout the late 1860s. Although the Crispins viewed the BLS as a consolation prize, many of the labor reformers hoped that careful study of working conditions in the Bay State would provide support for their arguments for an eight-hour workday. The governor likely disappointed the labor reformers by his choice of Henry K. Oliver, who had close ties to the state's textile manufactures, to head the new agency. However, Oliver then chose George McNeill, Steward's ally in the eight-hour movement, to be his deputy, and McNeill hired Mary Bowers Steward, the eight-hour leader's wife, as his secretary.

Under Oliver and McNeill, the BLS functioned in many ways as a labor reform organization. In its first annual report, published in March 1870, it called for a ten-hour law in factories, stricter controls over child labor, and safer working conditions. Revealing their sympathies, the report's authors declared that "the wage system, ... which has been to the present day, the accepted method of distribution of the proceeds of labor, has proved to be adverse in its influence to the general good, and ... ought to yield to the system of cooperation." The BLS continued to operate as an advocate for the working class for three more years. Then, in 1873, less as a result of opposition from employers than as a consequence of internal divisions within the state's labor reform movement, Oliver and McNeill were dismissed. Their replacement, Carroll Wright, was a patent attorney and former state senator who had few connections to the labor reform campaign. Wright would remain as director of the BLS for fifteen years, and his reports tended to avoid bold policy recommendations.

Failure on the eight-hour front stimulated labor reformers and activists in Massachusetts to organize a cross-class independent labor reform political party, and in September 1869, at a convention in Worcester, the Massachusetts Labor Reform Party (MLRP) was born. Ira Steward, who along with George McNeill and other labor activists had recently formed the Boston Eight Hour League, attended the convention along with trade unionists and industrial workers. The party's platform endorsed both shorter hours and currency reform, what was known as greenbackism. Looking to go beyond petitions and lobbying, the MLRP embraced third-party politics in the upcoming elections. With the veteran reformer Edwin Chamberlain running for governor on its ticket, the new party amassed more than 13,000 votes or 10 percent of the total cast and elected twenty legislative candidates.

The following year, the MLRP chose Wendell Phillips as its nominee for governor. Phillips had come to believe that the ballot box afforded workers the best means of self-protection against the influence of large-scale capital in politics. Although he had "no wish" to be governor, Phillips accepted that "to rally a political party, disinterested men must give years to the work of enlightening the public mind and organizing their ranks." He exhorted workers to "write over the ballot-box, 'Here we never forgive!' ... Why? Because the great object of a class, when they have a claim on the community, is to be understood. Do not be equivocal." Despite the Labor Reform Party's high hopes for Phillips, he polled a disappointing 12 percent of the vote. Encouraging the labor party to stay together, he told the 1871 convention, "You do not destroy the virus of incorporated wealth by any one election." But Phillips and Steward had an acrimonious falling out one year later, and the Labor Reform Party was itself splintering.

Building a National Organization

An eight-hour workday law was one of the pivotal labor reform issues that drew sixty-five delegates from local and national unions in twenty different trades along with leaders and middle-class labor reformers representing Eight Hour Leagues to Baltimore in 1866 to form the National Labor Union. Although founded by the trade unionists as a labor organization, the NLU was never granted the standard powers assigned to national craft unions of the boycott, strike support, or arbitration. Moreover, since each member union retained absolute autonomy, the NLU never became a truly national labor union during the five years that it existed. The majority of the delegates who traveled to Baltimore and to subsequent NLU congresses were members of local and city trade bodies. An "Address to Workingmen" that was issued in 1867 after the Chicago NLU congress by a five-member committee led by Andrew Carr Cameron, the editor of the *Workingman's Advocate*, outlined the national union's platform. In it, the NLU endorsed the formation of cooperatives, a shortening of the workday, and the thorough organization of workingmen and workingwomen into trade unions; it also recognized a need to organize "Negro" workers. At the Baltimore convention, J. C. C. Whaley, a leader in the typographical union in Washington, DC, and Edward Schlaeger, representing the German Workingmen's Association of Chicago, were elected as the NLU's first president and vice president, respectively, but neither was appropriated a salary and no real central administrative structure was created.

Because of illness, Sylvis was unable to attend the founding NLU convention. After the Baltimore convention he commented that the NLU's failure to develop a comprehensive organizational plan was a serious defect that he hoped would be remedied at the next meeting in Chicago. Although the second convention did adopt a constitution, it would not be until Sylvis was himself elected president in 1868 that a real effort was made to upgrade the NLU's adminstrative structure. Under Sylvis's guidance, the NLU established a system of salaried officials (Sylvis would receive $1,500 and expenses) and appointed executives in each state who would then appoint a subcommittee of five to organize locals. Sylvis's NLU also fixed membership qualifications and developed a mechanism for the collection of membership dues. In addition, the NLU executive committee authorized Sylvis to "canvass the principal cities and towns of the country for the purpose of discussing and disseminating the principles of the National Labor Union, and forming branch Unions." Following this mandate, Sylvis undertook a three-month tour of the South during which he organized twenty-six branches of the NLU, as well as reorganized suspended IMIU locals and established new ones.

At the 1868 NLU convention in New York City conflict arose over the issue of women's rights. Three women attended as delegates – Mary Kellogg Putnam (Working Women's Association No. 2 of New York City), the noted women's rights activist Susan B. Anthony (Working Women's Association No. 1 of New York City), and Mary A. McDonald (Working Women's Protective Labor Union of Mount Vernon, New York, No. 6). When Elizabeth Cady Stanton presented credentials from a woman suffrage organization and not a labor body, the mostly male delegates loudly protested and called for her eviction from the hall. Sylvis made a stirring speech in support of sitting Stanton. She had, he asserted, "done more than anybody I know to elevate her class and my class too, and God knows they need elevation." The convention accepted Stanton's credentials but only under the proviso that the NLU was not thereby endorsing "her peculiar ideas." However, the convention did adopt the committee on female labor's report which recommended that the eight-hour workday be established for women workers, that there be equal pay for equal work, and that women's trade unions be organized. Sylvis then appointed Kate Mullany, who had organized the laundresses in Troy into a union, to be a special NLU assistant secretary in charge of coordinating national efforts to form workingwomen's associations. In his closing remarks to the convention, Sylvis noted that the NLU now had a female officer and he expressed the hope that in the future the organization would have delegates representing the nation's 300,000 workingwomen.

Mullany and the Molders' Union president had become allies before the 1868 NLU convention. An immigrant from Ireland, Mullany had gone to work in the mid-1860s in a commercial laundry in the upstate New York city of Troy, where 90 percent of the shirts, collars, and cuffs worn by middle-class men in the United States were produced. More than 3,000 women, almost half of the city's female industrial workforce, worked in the collar industry. Being a laundress was considered to be a good job; nevertheless, the women labored under harsh conditions, washing, boiling, bleaching, and starching shirt collars, while earning only $3 to $4 a week (the lowest wages in the industry), minus any deductions if they damaged a shirt or collar.

In 1864, with the encouragement of the local Iron Molders' Union, Mullany and a coworker, Esther Keegan, successfully organized about 300 women into the Troy Collar Laundry Union. A five-day strike in February of that year won the workers a 20 percent to 25 percent wage increase. Two years later, after a short strike, the union once again won a pay increase. But then, in 1869, following the example of the stove manufacturers, the laundry owners formed a coalition with the collar manufacturers to kill the union. During the long strike that followed, the union attempted to form a cooperative, the Union Line Collar and Cuff Manufactory. Despite some initial success both the cooperative and the strike failed, and in February 1870 Mullany and the other officers dissolved the laundresses' union. After the strike, Mullany moved into a house her mother bought on Eighth Street in Troy, where she died in 1906.

During his organizing tour of the South, Sylvis frequently expressed a deep-seated racism that was common among white workers. Even so, he recognized that the whole laboring population – white and African American – had to be united if only to ensure that the "blacks" would not be used against the labor movement in the South: "If workmen of the white race do not conciliate the blacks, the blacks will vote against them" and serve as strikebreakers. In the 1867 "Address to Workingmen" Cameron had insisted that the labor movement should make no distinctions by race or nationality. There was but one dividing line, the "one which separates mankind into two great classes, the class that labors and the class that lives by others' labor." Although Sylvis agreed with Cameron about the urgency for class solidarity, internal divisions aroused by racism and fears of job competition led the NLU to evade the issue of organizing African American workers.

The postbellum South that Sylvis toured had a formidable black working class. Before the war, both slaves and free black laborers were employed in Richmond's Tredegar Iron Works, in the tobacco industry, in brick making, in ship caulking, and in railway construction, as well as on the docks. In Charleston, South Carolina, where free blacks worked in many skilled occupations, the *African Repository* claimed that in Charleston, "in some cases," the African Americans "have no competitors." According to one estimate, after the Civil War the number of black mechanics was five times that of white mechanics in the South.

Early in 1867, as a strike wave swept the South, black long-shoremen in Charleston formed the Longshoremen's Protective Union Association and won a strike for higher wages. In February black dock workers in Savannah, Georgia, went out on strike and won their demand that the city council repeal a poll tax of $10 on all persons employed on the wharves. The rapid growth of black labor organizations led to a call for the formation of central labor bodies. On July 19, 1869, delegates gathered in Baltimore to organize a statewide labor association. A local caulker, Isaac Myers, explained in his welcoming address that such an organization was needed not only because the existing trade unions frequently barred black mechanics from membership but also because self-organization was their best hope for improving their living standards. Agreeing with Myers, the delegates at the

Baltimore convention decided both to press for admission to the existing trade unions and to organize separate black unions.

In 1869 nine black delegates, including Myers, attended the NLU convention in New York, and the convention that year adopted a plan for organizing black workers. Myers spoke of the need for unity and proclaimed that what black workers most desired was an equal opportunity to labor under conditions similar to those of white workers. The black caulker observed that black workers, like their white counterparts, wished to obtain wages that would "secure them a comfortable living for their families, educate their children, and leave a dollar for a rainy day and for old age." In his address, Myers expressed the hope that the NLU would develop into a coalition of white and black labor.

Although Sylvis had expressed his belief that a well-run campaign could unite the whole laboring population of the South behind the platform of the NLU, the labor organization never adopted a policy of racial integration. Many of the member trade unions resisted permitting black mechanics to enter their ranks and supported instead the formation of "Jim Crow," or racially separate, locals. In May 1869 the son of Frederick Douglass was given a job with the Government Printing Office (GPO) in Washington, DC. He then applied for but was denied membership in the Columbia Typographical Union. Without discussion the next International Typographical Union's convention voted to censure the GPO for employing Douglass. The hostility of white craft NLU unions to black workers led, in November 1869, to the formation of the Colored National Labor Union (CNLU). Declaring that African American workers were "[f]orced to endure wrongs and oppression worse than Slavery," a call to organize a national labor convention went out in the black press and was echoed from the pulpits of black churches. The convention's promoters looked to bring together the "colored" workingmen of the several states to act cooperatively in a separate organization.

More than 200 delegates, whose ranks included African American ministers, merchants, attorneys, carpenters, tailors, and other (including some white) workingmen, attended the inaugural convention of the CNLU, which was held in Washington. Aimed at fostering black trade organizations, the CNLU brought together black unionists and black political leaders. It opposed discrimination against African Americans and their exclusion from trades as "an insult to God." Its platform called for black workers in every state to establish cooperative workshops, pursue education, avoid the "evil of intemperance," and form workingmen's associations. After the convention, Isaac Myers, who had been elected the CNLU's first president, went out on an organizing tour through the South. In Norfolk, Virginia, Myers advised a group of African Americans that the "watchword of the colored men must be organize!" Unlike the delegates to the NLU, who were mainly skilled artisans and mechanics, the membership of the CNLU also included industrial, agricultural, and common laborers, both men and women.

Even after the formation of the CNLU, black delegates continued to attend the annual NLU meetings. At the fourth NLU convention in Cincinnati in 1870 bitter disputes erupted over the seating of a black delegate because of his affiliation with the Republican Party and over a resolution that asked "our colored fellow citizens" to abandon the existing political parties, which were considered to be dominated by financial capitalists. Although Myers acknowledged that the Republican Party was not the "*beau idéal* of our notion of a party," he nevertheless insisted that the interests of the working man would not be advanced by the organization of a new party or by affiliation with the Democratic Party. In the end, all of the black delegates voted against a resolution supporting the formation of an independent labor reform party. The 1870 NLU convention would be the last one attended by black delegates.

In January 1871 the CNLU held its second meeting in Washington. In his keynote speech Myers asserted that because capital was better organized and more powerful financially, the organizing of trade unions was essential "for advancing the claims and protecting the interests of the workmen." Myers hoped that the CNLU would concentrate on the building of trade unions rather than on engaging in politics, which he believed would only be divisive. As a testament to the growing importance of black political leaders, the convention replaced Myers as president of the CNLU with Frederick Douglass. Under Douglass's leadership, action on behalf of the labor and economic goals of the CNLU program faded as the organization concentrated on political action, especially in support of the Republican Party. After 1871, perhaps as much a result of the forces arrayed against it as of the CNLU's move toward political engagement, the black labor organization would never meet again.

The resolution passed at its 1870 convention to form an independent labor-based party would also have fateful consequences for the NLU. How workingmen could best use their collective voting power was not a new issue. In the mid-1860s Sylvis and the IMIU faced a counterattack from organized capital. Though never abandoning his belief in the need for workers to organize themselves in unions, he also sought some means of securing "permanent relief" beyond labor organization and the strike. "The fact is," Sylvis pointed out, "if every working man in America was a good law-abiding member of his union we would still be subject to the whims and caprice of capitalists." After the Baltimore NLU convention in 1866, Sylvis, who had long been ambivalent about organizing an independent labor party, wrote that the "history of broken promises" and "deceptions" by candidates for political office had convinced him "that if we resort to political action at all, we must keep clear of all entangling alliances. … If labor had its own political party … workingmen can vote for men *of* them and *with* them." Despite the support expressed for the formation of an independent labor party, nothing concrete was agreed to in Baltimore. The following year the NLU convention adopted a vague resolution but no formal plan of action was offered. By 1868, Sylvis had become convinced that most of the "evils under which we groan" were the result of "bad laws" that could be cured only "by repeal" and this required "political action." Thus, after the 1868 convention, which had established a committee to draw up a platform for a proposed national labor party, the NLU president endeavored to put together the administrative structure of the new party. He even expressed the hope that labor would "make the president in 1872."

Modeled on the Declaration of Independence, the Declaration of Principles drawn up after the 1868 NLU convention highlighted the growing significance of greenbackism, ideas about "soft money." The basic concepts of currency reform were first introduced in the late 1840s by the businessman and self-taught economist Edward Kellogg and were updated two decades later by Alexander Campbell, a member of the NLU, in *A True American System of Finance* (1864). At the top of the political agenda pursued by Sylvis and other leaders of the NLU was reform of the nation's monetary system, especially the reissuing of legal-tender treasury notes, or greenbacks, as the exclusive US currency. But, despite their leaders' support for political action to achieve this and other goals, many delegates representing the trade unions opposed labor's turn to politics. The split between the trade unionists and the supporters of labor politics came to a head when the executive committee for the new National Labor Reform Party (NLRP) was selected and authorized to set a date for a convention to nominate candidates. As a result, the NLU divided into two organizations, a "political" group that launched the NLRP and sought to nominate candidates for political office, and an "industrial" faction which then took control of the NLU.

The NLRP held its founding convention in February 1872 in Columbus, Ohio. After passing a platform that called on the federal government to continue printing limited amounts of paper money, the convention nominated Judge David Davis, Lincoln's former campaign manager and a Supreme Court justice, to run for president. Davis eventually withdrew as a candidate, and the NLRP then endorsed the Democratic candidate, who received fewer than 30,000 votes in the election. Meanwhile, the 1872 convention of the "industrial" wing of the NLU attracted only seven delegates. Thus, even before the panic of 1873 would devastate labor reform efforts, the first postwar attempt to build a national labor movement had collapsed.

In Massachusetts, although labor historians debate the degree to which Wendell Phillips had, by the early 1870s, become a greenbacker, the issue of currency reform may have contributed to the 1872 breakup of the labor reform alliance of Ira Steward and Phillips. In May of that year Steward directed the Eight Hour League to censure Phillips, charging that the patrician reformer's expansive rhetoric and reform agenda were "distracting public and political attention" from the shortening of the workday. To Steward, who could not countenance any deviation from his eight-hour dogma, Phillips's endorsement of a broad labor reform agenda made him an apostate to the cause. Recently, however, a labor historian has pointed to the so-called Chinese question, which flared in Massachusetts in the early 1870s, as the basis for the growing animosity between Steward and Phillips. In the summer of 1870 a North Adams shoe manufacturer employed seventy-three Chinese immigrants, who were derided as "coolies," as strikebreakers. Steward had long railed against the importation of "cheap labor, such as that performed by the coolies." Leaders of the labor movement in Massachusetts led protests against "those who would reduce American workers to the Chinese standard of rice and rats." Phillips condemned such rhetoric as bigotry: "Have you so poorly learned the

Declaration that you are going at this hour to take up the old cries of 'race,' and 'America for the Americans?'" After Phillips and other reformers split with the Eight Hour League, the organization endorsed a ban on the migration of "coolie labor" to America.

The internal battles within the American labor movement over gender, race, politics, and the nature of its agenda that surfaced in the early 1870s were exacerbated in 1873 by a national economic crisis. Economic panic, precipitated by the collapse of the banking house of Jay Cooke and Company on September 18, 1873, which was quickly followed by the crash of other financial firms, rapidly spread across the country from the East Coast to engulf all forms of enterprise. By 1874 fully a million workers were without jobs nationwide. In New York City an estimated 25 percent of all workers were unemployed, and those who were able to hold on to their jobs found their wages severely cut. As the numbers of unemployed grew so too did calls for relief. Inevitably, violent confrontations occurred. In New York a group known as the Committee of Safety demanded that the city aid jobless workers by enlarging public works projects and by suspending home evictions of the unemployed during the winter months. On January 13, 1874, 7,000 unemployed workers rallying in Tompkins Square Park were surrounded by police, who, wielding their wooden clubs indiscriminately, cleared the park and the surrounding area of protesters and their supporters. Looking back, the labor leader Samuel Gompers expressed his horror at the "orgy of brutality" inflicted by the police: "To this day I cannot think of that wild scene without my blood surging in indignation at the brutality of the police on that day." Rejecting any social responsibility for the poor, the elite even went so far as to argue for the positive impact of the depression. Expressing a "survival of the fittest" Darwinian logic, they extolled the virtue of the crisis which, by weeding out inefficient businesses, would enable only the firms that were fiscally strong to live on. The industry journal *Iron Age* observed that another "positive side" to the economic crisis was that "the power of the trade unions for mischief is weakened." The conflict over the unemployed that came to a head in Tompkins Square in New York in 1874 demonstrated on a small scale the confrontation that took place on a national scale a few years later during the Great Railroad Strike of 1877.

A Tradition of Labor Protest Persists

The economic disorder caused by the panic of 1873 continued unabated through much of the decade. By 1876 not only had the Northern Pacific Railroad failed as a consequence of the unrestrained speculation of Jay Cooke and Company, but, having defaulted on their bonds, half of the nation's railroads were in receivership. This financial disaster ended the railroad boom that had fueled industrial expansion. Between 1867 and 1873 railroad companies had laid some 35,000 miles of track across the United States. But the severe cutbacks in track construction by the end of 1874 contributed to a suspension of operations in half of the nation's iron furnaces. The bottom was reached in 1878 when some 10,000 businesses failed and wholesale prices stood at only 30 percent of their level five years earlier.

Steady work also quickly disappeared, and by 1877–78 some three million US workers were unemployed. Among those who did find jobs, fewer than one-fifth worked continuously, and double that number labored for no more than six or seven months in the year. And those who worked did so for lower wages and longer hours. Whereas a skilled craftsman in the building trades in

The Dawning of American Labor: The New Republic to the Industrial Age,
First Edition. Brian Greenberg.

New York City was paid $2.50 to $3.00 for an eight-hour day in 1872, by 1875 he could earn only $1.50 to $2.00 for a ten-hour day. Likewise, the wages of textile workers in the nation fell by 45 percent, and railway workers experienced a cut of 30 to 40 percent during these years.

Hard times virtually wiped out the impressive gains that organized labor had made during the previous decade. Prior to the panic, workers founded thirty national unions; by 1877 only eight or nine remained. And those that survived were gravely weakened. The national machinists' and blacksmiths' union lost two-thirds of its members, and the typographers' union more than half. Local union membership in the nation's industrial cities experienced comparable losses. In New York City union membership declined from about 45,000 workers in 1873 to 5,000 in 1878; in the same year, Cleveland, which had been a thriving union town before the panic, became a largely nonunion city. Overall, contemporary estimates indicate that national union membership fell from about 300,000 in 1873 to about 50,000 six years later.

Workers' resistance to their employers persisted after 1873, but unions now often found themselves confronting a more highly organized capitalist class. In Albany and Troy the stove founders viewed the postpanic economic depression as an opportunity to try again to break the iron molders' union. In 1877, stating that they already had a surplus of stoves in stock, the owners declared that they would not reopen their foundries, which were normally closed during the winter months, in the coming spring unless the price of labor was cut; moreover, they asserted that they could hire anyone they wanted, set wage scales with each individual worker, and employ as many apprentices as they deemed best. Certain that the molders would reject their terms, the founders began locking out the workers and arranging for replacement molders from Canada. One Albany founder, Perry and Company, contracted with officials at Sing Sing Prison in Ossining, New York, to have a branch foundry opened at the state institution. In May 1877, confronted by their employers' united opposition and unable to stave off defeat, the iron molders' union suspended its rules for six months, thereby allowing members to return to work without appearing to be strikebreakers.

Like the Great Strike of 1877 on the railroads, developments in the coal industry foreshadowed the bitter confrontations between labor and capital during the final two decades of the nineteenth century. In the anthracite or hard coal industry in Pennsylvania, the Irish-born labor leader John Siney founded the Workingmen's Benevolent Association (WBA) of Schuylkill County in 1868. This union quickly grew to represent some 20,000 Irish, British, and American miners in twenty-two districts in the state. The WBA established a sick and death benefits fund, promoted the formation of cooperatives, and favored the use of arbitration to settle labor disputes. In 1870 the union signed its first contract with the coal operators, who agreed to a sliding-scale wage formula that would stabilize the industry in the county until 1874.

Despite the WBA's growth, Siney turned his attention away from the union to politics, lobbying for mine safety laws and, in 1871, helping to organize a labor party in Pennsylvania. Around this time miners in the bituminous or soft coal industry expressed interest in forming a national union of their own. The Miners' National Union of America (MNA), founded in October 1873, gained about 25,000 members in its first year. The next year, Siney moved to Cleveland to serve as president of the MNA. Hoping to avoid strikes while the union was growing, Siney advised the miners to exercise caution even as the mine operators were cutting their wages. But the membership ignored him and went out on strike, demanding that the MNA pay them weekly benefits. By 1875 the MNA treasury was nearly bankrupt.

The failure of trade unionism in the coal industry was more than just another casualty of the 1873 panic and the economic depression that followed. It was the direct result of an antiunion campaign led by Franklin B. Gowen, the president of the Philadelphia and Reading Railroad and its subsidiary, the Philadelphia and Reading Coal Company. Gowen, much like John D. Rockefeller in the oil industry and Andrew Carnegie in steel, sought to establish monopolistic power by gaining control of the market in the railroad industry. Gowen prepared well for his offensive against the union, importing contract labor to work in the mines and hiring company police and labor spies. Having bought out the Schuylkill coal operators who opposed his drive against the union, Gowen in December 1874 announced a series of wage cuts and demanded that the minimum wage be eliminated. As a way of undercutting the WBA, he also established benefit programs for the miners he employed. His objective according to union leaders was "not against wages so much as it was 'directly against our organization.'"

In these years the Molly Maguires, a violent Irish nationalist group committed to the idea of retributive justice, was also active in the Pennsylvania coalfields. Convinced that the Mollies were merely the terrorist arm of the union movement and anxious to destroy the power of both, in 1873 Gowen hired the private detective Alan Pinkerton. Pinkerton assigned James McParlan to the coal area. McParlan's job was to infiltrate the Mollies and gather information against both them and the labor movement. After two and a half years under cover, McParlan fled the area. Gowen's private police force arrested many members of the Molly Maguires, and McParlan became the chief prosecution witness against them in a series of trials that began in 1876. Remarkably, Gowen, a lawyer, served as the prosecutor at several of the trials. Eventually, twenty Molly Maguires were found guilty and hanged.

In 1875, while McParlan was still infiltrating the Molly Maguires, the WBA, now known as the Miners' and Laborers' Benevolent Association (MLBA), was engaged in the "long strike," a six-month struggle against the anthracite mine operators that was led by John F. Walsh, an English miner. Gowen's antiunion campaign was facilitated by the Pennsylvania governor's agreement to send in state troops to break the strike. After only a few months, the anthracite miners in Schuylkill County, who had refused to join the MLBA, voted to accept the wage cuts and to return to work. With few resources to sustain the strikers and a split in the ranks, "the long strike" ended in a total defeat for the miners. Walsh and other MLBA leaders were forced to leave the area, and the union disbanded. The convictions of the Molly Maguires a year later meant that Gowen's power was finally absolute.

By the mid-1880s coal miners were again organizing but now as part of the Knights of Labor (KOL). The Noble and Holy Order of the Knights of Labor had been founded in 1869 by a group of Philadelphia tailors. Under the leadership of their grand master workman Uriah S. Stephens, who in 1862 had helped organize the Garment Cutters' Association of Philadelphia, the Knights functioned, in their early years, less as a labor organization and more as a fraternal society. As such a society, the Knights were committed to ritual and secrecy. Stephens was critical of craft union organization and insisted that labor could meet the power of capital only by uniting all workers – including women and African Americans – regardless of skill. Unity would be achieved through secrecy, which protected members from their employers; through the gradual substitution of cooperative for capitalist production; and through education, which would help break down the preconceptions and antagonism that kept workers apart. Open to all manual workers, the Knights organized workers from a single craft into trade assemblies and created mixed assemblies that brought together workers from several different occupations. By minimizing craft exclusiveness, the mixed assemblies promoted solidarity and a broader social identity among workers. By the time they held their first national convention in 1878 in Reading,

Pennsylvania, the Knights had begun its transition from a fraternal society to a federation of industrial workers.

The Knights' Reading convention endorsed a statement of principles that resonated with the ideal of America as a producers' republic, an ideal that could be traced back to the early nineteenth century. Calling attention to the "recent alarming development and aggressiveness of aggregated wealth," whose power could be checked only by the widespread organization of workers, the Knights set up a general assembly to elect officers and decide all matters of policy. Echoing William Sylvis's conviction that, to find permanent relief, "We must adopt such means as will strike down the whole system of wages for labor," the Knights dedicated themselves to organizing "every department of productive industry" with the aim of replacing the wage system through the formation of "co-operative institutions, productive and distributive." In excluding from membership society's "nonproducers" or "parasites" – bankers, speculators, lawyers, and liquor dealers – the KOL fought to preserve the independence of the "producing classes" – workers, farmers, and honorable manufacturers. Adopting measures that they believed would abolish "wage slavery," the Knights endorsed the eight-hour workday, the end of the convict labor system, and the substitution of arbitration for strikes whenever an employer and his employees were willing "to meet on equitable grounds." In addition, the KOL called for equal pay for equal work and for laws ending child (under the age of fourteen) labor. In 1879 Terence Powderly, a machinist who had joined the Knights five years earlier, was elected grand master workman to replace Stephens, who had resigned the previous year to run, unsuccessfully, for Congress as a nominee of the Greenback-Labor Party.

Greenbackism resurfaced briefly in the mid-1870s as a political movement. The violent engagement of federal troops suppressing the railway strikers in 1877 convinced many in labor that government was hostile to its aims. Political parties emerged in a number of industrial centers. In Pennsylvania, greenbackers attended an August 1877 conference of the United Labor Party, which had been recently organized by trade unions. Following the conference, the two groups agreed to merge their forces into what the press called the Greenback Party. Fusion also occurred in Ohio, where workingmen organized a national party that called for the substitution of greenbacks for all US bank notes and the remonetization of silver. The fusion movements in Pennsylvania polled nearly 10 percent of the vote in 1877, and in Toledo, Ohio, a whole workingmen's municipal ticket was swept into office; two assemblymen were also elected to the Ohio state legislature. In Massachusetts, Wendell Phillips was again speaking out in support of greenback reform. In an 1878 article published in *The Outlook*, Phillips pointed out that all the Greenback Party was trying to do was "develop an American system of finance," one that represented a revolt against the notion that "in ordinary matters the people can govern themselves, but on questions of finance they must be kept under perpetual guardianship, and be the wards of rich men."

The early success of the greenback–labor coalition led to a call for a national convention to meet in February 1878 in Toledo. In addition to currency reform, the Greenback-Labor Party endorsed reduced hours of labor, the formation of national and state bureaus of labor statistics, and the prohibition of convict labor; in addition, it opposed the importation of "servile labor." In the fall elections the party elected mayors in a number of communities, including Terence Powderly, as mayor of Scranton, Pennsylvania. In congressional elections across the nation, fourteen candidates from the Greenback-Labor Party were elected; overall, the party polled more than a million votes. Yet the 1878 election would represent the high-water mark for the greenback–labor movement. Labor and agrarian interests in the party fought over the party's aims, and, although a national convention in 1880 was well-attended, in that year's national election few workers appear to have voted for James B. Weaver, the party's nominee for president.

In 1881 the Knights dropped the practice of secrecy and began to expand rapidly. But the KOL eventually became a casualty of a government-supported capital counteroffensive that followed the massive strike wave in 1886 known as the Great Upheaval. In that same year, however, the national trade unions representing native-born skilled craft workers organized the American Federation of Labor (AFL) as a loose alliance among themselves. The new federation chose Samuel Gompers, a leader of the Cigar Makers' International Union since the late 1870s, as its first president. Critical of the Knights' more inclusive membership and expansive social vision, the AFL under Gompers practiced pure and simple "business unionism." Gompers saw trade unions as "voluntary associations of wage-earners" that could satisfy workers' "bread and butter" needs through collective bargaining with employers. Gompers had come to believe that opposition by the labor movement to the concentration of corporate economic power in the United States was futile. To be effective, workers had to fashion trade unions as counterorganizations capable of dealing with capital on an equal footing. This would not happen, in Gompers's view, until the unions centralized authority and developed a practical administrative system in addition to maintaining their focus on winning tangible benefits for their members. Only when trade unions achieved a balance of power with capital could they, through collective bargaining, secure members' material needs: higher wages, shorter hours, and better working conditions. The alternative perspectives on labor organization advanced by the Knights and the AFL during the 1870s and 1880s were just the latest expression of the divergent nature of nineteenth-century working-class consciousness. These differences were very much in evidence during the first workers' holiday celebration, the 1882 Labor Day parade in New York City.

From that day forward, much of the writing on the beginnings of Labor Day in the United States has focused on designating a "father" of the workers' holiday. Gompers singled out Peter J. McGuire, a leader of the United Brotherhood of Carpenters and Joiners and a co-founder of the AFL, as the "undisputed author of Labor Day as a holiday." Yet other labor leaders have insisted that the honor belonged to Matthew Maguire (they were not related), a secretary of the Knights' machinists' and blacksmiths' local in Brooklyn, New York, and an activist in the eight-hour labor movement. The labor historians Michael Kazin and Steven J. Ross have appropriately dubbed the "father" controversy a "minor question," one that they insist downplays the day's true significance as a public ritual during which working people collectively expressed "their needs, fears, and aspirations."

The day's events were organized by the Central Labor Union (CLU), a New York City umbrella body formed by labor activists, socialists, skilled craftsmen, industrial operatives from diverse backgrounds, and supporters of the Knights of Labor. Established in November 1881 to, in the words of one printer, replace the "'narrow-minded view of the interests of a single occupation' with that of 'the general interests of all bodies of wage workers,'" the CLU was led by Robert Blissert, a New York tailor and a member of the Knights of Labor Local 1563 in New York City, as well as by Peter McGuire and Matthew Maguire. On May 14 the CLU proposed a "monster" labor festival to take place in early September. A committee of five was appointed to make the necessary arrangements, and on August 6 the date of September 5 was chosen for a general holiday for the workingmen of the city. This date coincided, not coincidentally, with a planned meeting in New York City of the KOL's general assembly. For the CLU, the day's events were intended to "show the strength and esprit de corps of the trade and Labor organizations" and to "warn politicians that they shall go no farther in pandering to the greed of monopoly and reducing the conditions of the masses." A day before the parade, its grand marshal William McCabe, echoing labor's long-held republican consciousness, said of the CLU's goals for the day, "We are entering a contest to recover the rights of workingmen and secure henceforth to the producer the fruits of his toil. The demonstration tomorrow is the review before the battle."

Yet the motives behind labor's planned holiday on September 5 were mixed. As Kazin and Ross note, "themes of accommodation and resistance were played out" as labor attempted to build "a class conscious movement while also affirming their loyalty to conceptions of American citizenship that muted class distinctions." Some marchers held aloft more militant banners that declared "Labor Creates All Wealth," "Labor Built This Republic, Labor Shall Rule It," and "The True Remedy is Organization and the Ballot," and others, expressing support for more immediate reforms, carried banners that proclaimed "Down With the Tenement System" and "Down With Convict Labor," as well as "Less Hours and More Pay." Most common was support for the eight-hour workday, such as the banner held aloft by the city's Cigar Makers' Union, "Eight Hours for Work, Eight Hours for Rest, and Eight Hours for Recreation." Yet, along with these banners, marchers also held aloft large American flags and the parade included a drum-and-fife corps that evoked the spirit of '76. Maguire would later sum up the more practical goals that the city's labor movement had hoped to achieve: "No festival of martial glory of warrior's renown is this. ... It is dedicated to Peace, Civilization and the triumphs of Industry. It is a demonstration of fraternity and the harbinger of a better age."

Although it was perhaps not quite as large as its organizers had hoped, on September 5, 1882, more than 10,000 trade unionists and labor supporters in New York City came together in the first Labor Day parade in the United States. The parade, which marched past a reviewing stand in Union Square Park, was followed by a picnic that drew somewhere between 15,000 and 50,000 celebrants to Wendel's Elm Park to engage in an afternoon and evening of singing, dancing, gaming, and, for some, drinking.

The larger reform goals and aspirations of Labor Day have faded through the years. Although it became a national holiday in 1894, today few parades are held and the day simply marks the beginning of the school year in many communities throughout the United States. But, in 1882, many of those who marched that day and amused themselves that night were inspired by what they saw as mutual objectives: that Labor Day would be a day of celebration of the manual producer, a demonstration that would impress both their employers and the compliant politicians who deferred to them, as well as a day of unity for the labor movement, a coming together of a heterogeneous working class in America that often expressed conflicting views on how best to counter the exploitation and fix the social problems brought about by industrialization.

The solidarity shown during Labor Day and the respectability of the holiday's participants were highlighted in the city's newspaper accounts. The *New York Times* said of those who marched that they did so in an "orderly and pleasant manner," and pointed out that "nearly all were well-clothed, and some wore attire of fashionable cut." The disciplined conduct of the men in line bore testimony to the fact that they "demanded recognition as law-abiding, peaceable citizens." The great majority smoked cigars, and "all seemed bent upon having a good time at the picnic grounds." Emphasizing unity and good fellowship, the *New York Herald* commented about the picnic that "Fellow-workers and their families sat together, joked together, and caroused together. ... American and English, Irish and German, they all hobnobbed and seemed on a friendly footing, as though the common cause had established a closer sense of brotherhood." The day's success led the CLU to make Labor Day an annual event. Other cities would follow suit, and by 1886 Labor Day celebrations were occurring in cities throughout the country.

But 1886 was also the year of the Great Upheaval. A strike wave on behalf of the eight-hour day engulfed more than 400,000 workers in towns and cities across America. More strikes occurred in that year than in any previous year in American history. Although the employers' counteroffensive, which followed in the wake of the Great Upheaval, would lead to the rapid decline of the KOL, the Knights' ideal of America as a producers' republic persisted into the twentieth century. Alongside the AFL's more narrowly focused wage-conscious agenda, a tradition of worker organization and commitment to preserving the dignity of labor – one that can be traced back to the cordwainers' and other unions in the early nineteenth century, to the workingmen's movement of the 1830s, to the Lowell Female Labor Reform Association in the 1840s, and to the trade union and labor reform efforts led by William Sylvis and the National Labor Union in the 1860s and 1870s – lived on.

BIBLIOGRAPHICAL ESSAY

General Labor and Working-Class History

This bibliographical essay is meant as a brief survey of the leading works in the field, with particular emphasis on the scholarship that informed the present volume. The best introduction to the study of labor history can be found in Eric Arnesen, ed., *Encyclopedia of U.S. Labor and Working-Class History* (New York: Routledge, 2007). The *Encyclopedia* is accessible online at http://disciplinas. stoa.usp.br/pluginfile.php/159608/mod_resource/content/1/U_S__ Labor_and_Working_Class_History__3_Vol_set.pdf. For teachers, classroom materials and other useful resources, as well as ongoing discussions on labor history issues, are available online at the website of the Labor and Working-Class History Association (www.LAW CHA.org) and at H-Labor (https://networks.h-net.org/h-labor). Three scholarly journals present the best in current labor history research. Published since 1960, *Labor History* reflects the older, more institutional approach to the study of labor history. Until 2007, *Labor History* issued an annual labor history bibliography; these are collected in Maurice F. Newfield, Daniel Leab, and Dorothy Swanson, eds., *American Working Class History: A Representative*

The Dawning of American Labor: The New Republic to the Industrial Age,
First Edition. Brian Greenberg.
© 2018 John Wiley & Sons, Inc. Published 2018 by John Wiley & Sons, Inc.

Bibliography (New York: Bowker, 1983). *Labor: Studies in Working-Class History of the Americas* takes a more social and cultural approach to the study of the evolving economic and political conditions of working-class history in the Americas. In the same vein but even more global in its approach is *International Labor and Working-Class History*. Each of these journals offers reviews of current scholarship and symposia devoted to outstanding works and important historiographic controversies.

A number of document collections are also essential to the student of labor history. Most important is the ten-volume documentary history of US industrial society from colonial times to 1880, John R. Commons et al., eds., *A Documentary History of American Industrial Society* (1910–11; repr. New York: Russell & Russell, 1958). More limited but still valuable are Albert Fried, ed., *Except to Walk Free: Documents and Notes in the History of American Labor* (Garden City, NY: Doubleday, 1974), and Philip S. Foner and Ronald L. Lewis, eds., *Black Workers: A Documentary History from Colonial Times to the Present* (Philadelphia: Temple University Press, 1989). On workers in early America there is Paul A. Gilje and Howard B. Rock, eds., *Keepers of the Revolution: New Yorkers at Work in the Early Republic* (Ithaca, NY: Cornell University Press, 1992). For documents on women and work, see Mary H. Blewett, *We Will Rise in Our Might: Workingwomen's Voices from Nineteenth-Century New England* (Ithaca, NY: Cornell University Press, 1991). Two nineteenth-century histories of labor that provide evidence of contemporary views are George E. McNeill, ed., *The Labor Movement: The Problem of Today* (1887; repr. New York: Augustus M. Kelley, 1971), and George A. Stevens, *New York Typographical Union No. 6: A Study of a Modern Trade Union and Its Predecessors* (Albany, NY: J. B. Lyon, 1913).

A number of studies of economic change from the late eighteenth century to the last quarter of the nineteenth century are very helpful in understanding the context of workers' response to industrialization in these years. Especially useful are George Rodgers Taylor, *The Transportation Revolution, 1815–1860* (New York: Harper & Row, 1951); Walter Licht, *Industrializing America: The Nineteenth Century* (Baltimore: Johns Hopkins University Press, 1995); John Lauritz Larson, *The Market Revolution in America: Liberty, Ambition, and the Eclipse of the Common Good* (New York: Cambridge University Press, 2010); Stuart Bruchey, *The Roots of American Economic Growth, 1607– 1861: An Essay in Social Causation* (New York: Harper Torchbooks, 1968); Douglass C. North, *The Economic Growth of the United States, 1790–1860* (New York: W. W. Norton, 1966); Thomas C. Cochran, *Frontiers of Change: Early Industrialism in America* (New York: Oxford University Press, 1981); James A. Henretta and Gregory H. Nobles, *Evolution and Revolution: American Society, 1600–1820* (Lexington, MA: D. C. Heath, 1987); and Gary J. Kornblith, ed., *The Industrial Revolution in America* (Boston: Houghton Mifflin, 1998). Also of value is an American history textbook produced by the American Social History Project under the direction of Herbert G. Gutman, *Who Built America? Working People and the Nation's Economy, Politics, Culture, and Society*, vol. 1 (New York: Pantheon Books, 1989).

Overview histories of labor offer an excellent introduction to the major events and key figures in the history of labor between 1787 and 1882. Of great value to the present volume has been Sean Wilentz, "The Rise of the American Working-Class, 1776–1877: A Survey," in *Perspectives on American Labor History: The Problems of Synthesis*, ed. J. Carroll Moody and Alice Kessler-Harris (DeKalb: Northern Illinois University Press, 1989), 83–151, and Bruce Laurie, *Artisans into Workers: Labor in Nineteenth-Century America* (New York: Hill & Wang, 1989). Standing out among earlier works are Joseph G. Rayback, *A History of American Labor* (New York: Free Press, 1966); Foster Rhea Dulles and Melvyn Dubofsky, *Labor in America: A History*,

4th ed. (Arlington Heights, IL: Harlan Davidson, 1984); Melvyn Dubofsky, *Industrialism and the American Worker, 1865–1920* (Arlington Heights, IL: Harlan Davidson, 1985); Dubofsky, "Labor Organizations," in *Encyclopedia of American Economic History: Studies of the Principal Movements and Ideas*, ed. Glenn Porter, vol. 2 (New York: Scribner's, 1980), 524–551; Richard O. Boyer and Herbert M. Morais, *Labor's Untold Story* (New York: United Electrical, Radio and Machine Workers of America, 1971); and James R. Green and Hugh Carter Donahue, *Boston's Workers, A Labor History* (Boston: Trustees of the Public Library of the City of Boston, 1979). More recent works that reflect the broadening of the study of labor history include Jacqueline Jones, *A Social History of the Laboring Classes: From Colonial Times to the Present* (Malden, MA: Blackwell, 1999); David Montgomery, *Citizen Worker: The Experience of Workers in the United States with Democracy and the Free Market during the Nineteenth Century* (New York: Cambridge University Press, 1994); Philip Dray, *There Is Power in a Union: The Epic Story of Labor in America* (New York: Doubleday, 2010); Philip Yale Nicholson, *Labor's Story in the United States* (Philadelphia: Temple University Press, 2004); Tom Juravich, William F. Hartford, and James R. Green, *Commonwealth of Toil: Chapters in the History of Massachusetts Workers and Their Unions* (Amherst: University of Massachusetts Press, 1996); and Richard Morris, ed., *The U.S. Department of Labor Bicentennial History of the American Worker*, at http://www.dol.gov/dol/aboutdol/history/amworker intro.htm.

Until the 1960s, the Wisconsin School was the prevailing approach to the study of labor history. Concentrating on the institutions and evolving structure of trade unions, the labor economists Richard T. Ely, John R. Commons, Selig Perlman, and their followers produced in the early twentieth century a vast body of work that provided a foundation for the study of labor history. See especially John R. Commons et al., *History of Labour in the*

United States, 4 vols. (New York: Macmillan, 1918–35). Perlman, a student of Commons, provided a theoretical framework for the Wisconsin School labor history in *A Theory of the Labor Movement* (1928; repr. New York: A. M. Kelley, 1968). Working somewhat outside the Commons tradition, Norman J. Ware wrote two major surveys of labor history, *The Industrial Worker, 1840–1860: The Reaction of American Industrial Society to the Advance of the Industrial Revolution* (Chicago: Quadrangle Books, 1964), and *The Labor Movement in the United States, 1860–1895* (1929; repr. Gloucester, MA: Peter Smith, 1959).

The most notable dissenter from the Wisconsin School before the 1960s was the historian Philip Foner. He too focused mainly on the actions of trade unions, strikes, and union politics, but, as a political radical, he did so as a critic rather than as a celebrant of the American Federation of Labor and the major trade unions. He took them to task for considering only the needs of skilled workers and for their neglect of African Americans, immigrants (in particular, Asians who came after 1880), women workers, and common laborers. A prolific author, Foner produced his own multivolume survey of labor history; see especially Philip S. Foner, *History of the Labor Movement in the United States,* vol. 1, *From Colonial Times to the Founding of the American Federation of Labor* (New York: International Publishers, 1978).

Beginning in the early 1960s, what became known as the "new" labor history began to displace the "old" labor history of Commons and his students. The flowering of new labor history among younger labor historians in the United States was influenced by the works of British social historians who examined the lives of the ordinary working people of England. E. P. Thompson's magisterial *The Making of the English Working Class* (New York: Vintage Books, 1963) was especially instrumental to the social history approach adopted by new labor historians. Thompson and his generation introduced the idea of a moral economy advanced by premodern workers during the early years of industrialization in England. See, in particular, Thompson's *Whigs and Hunters: The Origins of the Black Act* (New York: Penguin Books, 1990); Douglas Hay, Peter Linebaugh, John G. Rule, E. P. Thompson, and Cal Winslow, *Albion's Fatal Tree: Crime and Society in Eighteenth-Century England* (New York: Pantheon Books, 1976); Eric Hobsbawm and George Rudé, *Captain Swing* (New York: W. W. Norton, 1968); Eric Hobsbawm, *Laboring Men: Studies in the History of Labour* (Garden City, NY: Anchor Books, 1967); Eric Hobsbawm, *Workers: Worlds of Labor* (New York: Pantheon Books, 1984); and Gareth Stedman Jones, *Languages of Class: Studies in English Working Class History, 1832–1982* (New York: Cambridge University Press, 1983).

Often energized by the decade's radical New Left protest movements, younger new labor historians were inspired by the work of Herbert G. Gutman, who has been credited with drawing the attention of labor history away from trade unions "to the communities where workers lived and fought" and, especially, with "teaching a generation of scholars to appreciate workers as makers of their own history." His numerous studies of smaller American cities and towns during the Gilded Age, collected in Herbert G. Gutman, *Work, Culture, and Society in Industrializing America: Essays in American Working-Class History* (New York: Alfred A. Knopf, 1976), and in Gutman, *Power and Culture: Essays on the American Working Class*, ed. Ira Berlin (New York: Pantheon Books, 1987), emphasize worker culture, that is, the rules and values that generated and guided workers' response to industrialism. Like Gutman, the first generation of new labor historians saw themselves as writing history "from the bottom up." Based in local studies of industrial cities and towns, initially in the Northeast and then across the United States, new labor history identifies American workers' response to industrialism as being rooted in their particular communities. Two excellent collections of articles that represent the early efforts of the new labor historians are Michael H. Frisch and Daniel J. Walkowitz, eds.,

Working-Class America: Essays on Labor, Community, and American Society (Urbana: University of Illinois Press, 1983), and Charles Stephenson and Robert Asher, eds., *Life and Labor: Dimensions of American Working-Class History* (Albany: State University of New York Press, 1986). Many of these essays were subsequently expanded by their authors into books, and examples of these works can be found throughout this bibliography, especially in the sections covering Chapters 2 and 3.

The approach of the new labor historians has been assessed in David Brody, "The Old Labor History and the New: In Search of an American Working Class," *Labor History* 20, no. 1 (Winter 1979): 111–126; Michael Kazin, "Struggling with the Class Struggle: Marxism and the Search for a Synthesis of U.S. Labor History," *Labor History* 28, no. 4 (Fall 1987): 497–514; David Montgomery, "To Study the People: The American Working Class," *Labor History* 21, no. 4 (Fall 1980): 485–512; and Walter Licht, "Labor and Capital and the American Community," *Journal of Urban History* 7, no. 2 (February 1981): 219–238. In 1984 a conference funded by the National Endowment for the Humanities (NEH) brought many of the first generation of new labor historians together in the hopes of forging a synthesis. Although the conference failed to inspire a "Making of the American Working Class," its papers were published in J. Carroll Moody and Alice Kessler-Harris, eds., *Perspectives on American Labor History: The Problem of Synthesis* (DeKalb: Northern Illinois University Press, 1989).

Looking at both workers and management, David Montgomery offers an alternative to the community studies approach utilized by new labor historians, one that begins with conflict on the shop floor. In *Workers' Control in America: Studies in the History of Work, Technology, and Labor Struggles* (New York: Cambridge University Press, 1979), Montgomery highlights the "manliness" of skilled workers as they struggle to preserve their control over their work. Eventually, he tries to achieve a synthesis of his workplace-based studies and the community approach of the new labor historians; see David Montgomery, *The Fall of the House of Labor: The Workplace, the State, and American Labor Activism, 1865–1925* (New York: Cambridge University Press, 1987).

The concentration in labor scholarship on male workers led Alice Kessler-Harris to challenge labor historians at the National Endowment for the Humanities (NEH) "Perspectives" conference to incorporate gender more fully into their work. An excellent starting point for an understanding of the importance of gender in the history of work and the working class is Alice Kessler-Harris's own *Out to Work: A History of Wage-Earning Women in the United States* (New York: Oxford University Press, 1982). Other valuable essay collections and overviews are Alice Kessler-Harris, *Women Have Always Worked: A Historical Overview* (Old Westbury, NY: Feminist Press, 1981); Carol Groneman and Mary Beth Norton, eds., *"To Toil the Livelong Day": America's Women at Work, 1780–1980* (Ithaca, NY: Cornell University Press, 1987); Barbara Mayer Wertheimer, *We Were There: The Story of Working Women in America* (New York: Pantheon Books, 1977); Ava Baron, ed., *Work Engendered: Toward a New History of American Labor* (Ithaca, NY: Cornell University Press, 1991); Philip Foner, *Women and the American Labor Movement: From the First Trade Unions to the Present* (New York: Free Press, 1979); and Milton Cantor and Bruce Laurie, eds., *Class, Sex, and the Woman Worker* (Westport, CT: Greenwood Press, 1977).

Rather than attempt in this volume to incorporate the extensive literature on plantation slavery, I decided to focus on the African American experience with industrial conditions in the South as well as in the North. Frederick Douglass's autobiography, *Narrative of the Life of Frederick Douglass: An American Slave, Written by Himself*, ed. David W. Blight (Boston: Bedford Books, 1993), provides the best introduction to these issues. See also Philip S. Foner, *Organized Labor and the Black Worker, 1619–1973* (New York: International Publishers, 1974);

Ronald L. Lewis, *Coal, Iron, and Slaves: Industrial Slavery in Maryland and Virginia, 1715–1865* (Westport, CT: Greenwood Press, 1979); Charles B. Dew, "Disciplining Slave Iron Workers in the Antebellum South," *American Historical Review* 79, no. 2 (April 1974): 393–418; Ira Berlin, *Slaves without Masters: The Free Negro in the Antebellum South* (New York: Pantheon Books, 1974); Jacqueline Jones, *Labor of Love, Labor of Sorrow: Black Women, Work and the Family, from Slavery to the Present* (New York: Vintage Books, 1986); Robert S. Starobin, *Industrial Slavery in the Old South* (New York: Oxford University Press, 1970); Richard C. Wade, *Slavery in the Cities* (New York: Oxford University Press, 1964); Peter J. Rachleff, *Black Labor in Richmond, 1865–1890* (Urbana: University of Illinois Press, 1989); Seth Rockman, *Scraping By: Wage Labor, Slavery, and Survival in Early Baltimore* (Baltimore: Johns Hopkins University Press, 2009); and Ira Berlin and Herbert G. Gutman, "Natives and Immigrants, Free Men and Slaves: Urban Workingmen in the Antebellum American South," *American Historical Review* 88, no. 5 (December 1983): 1175–1200.

Prologue: American Exceptionalism and the Great Strike of 1877

A wonderful introduction to the historical significance of the Great Strike is provided by *1877: The Grand Army of Starvation*, a documentary video produced by the American Social History Project (a preview is available at http://ashp.cuny.edu/ashp-documentaries/eighteen-seventy-seven). The most comprehensive study of the Great Strike is Robert V. Bruce, *1877: Year of Violence* (Chicago: Quadrangle Books, 1959). An analysis of the Great Strike as the first mass insurgency movement in America can be found in Jeremy Brecher, *Strike!* (San Francisco: Straight Arrow Books, 1972). Other studies to consult on the strike's significance are Nick Salvatore, "Railway Workers and the Great Strike of

1877," *Labor History* 21, no. 4 (Fall 1980): 522–545; David O. Stowell, *Streets, Railroads, and the Great Strike of 1877* (Chicago: University of Chicago Press, 1999); and Samuel Yellen, *American Labor Struggles, 1877–1934* (New York: Monad Press, 1936). More recent scholarly works stimulated by the strike are David O. Stowell, ed., *The Great Strikes of 1877: New Perspectives on a Pivotal Moment in U.S. History* (Urbana: University of Illinois Press, 2008), and Troy Rondinone, "'History Repeats Itself': The Civil War and the Meaning of Labor Conflict in the Late Nineteenth Century," *American Quarterly* 59, no. 2 (June 2007): 397–419. Of particular value to understanding the Great Strike in the context of Reconstruction is Eric Foner, *Reconstruction: America's Unfinished Revolution, 1863–1877* (New York: Harper & Row, 1988). The role of the 1877 railway strike in the evolution of Eugene Debs's social and political beliefs is explained in Nick Salvatore, *Eugene V. Debs: Citizen and Socialist* (Urbana: University of Illinois Press, 1982).

In 1906 a German socialist, Werner Sombart, published his investigation into the working-class movement in America, *Why Is There No Socialism in the United States?*, edited and with an introductory essay by C. T. Husbands, foreword by Michael Harrington (White Plains, NY: M. E. Sharpe, 1976). Essentially, Sombart explained the distinctive social, political, and economic qualities of the American experience, or "American exceptionalism," as a consequence of the success of capitalism. According to Sombart, the superior material conditions experienced by American workers over their European counterparts meant that "socialistic utopias of every sort" foundered in the United States, "on the reefs of roast beef and apple pie." Since 1906 the question Sombart posed has been the subject of an extended debate among scholars and historians of American labor and radical history. This historical debate is perceptively reviewed in Eric Foner, "Why Is There No Socialism in the United States?," *History Workshop* 17 (Spring 1984): 57–80; and in Sean Wilentz, "Against

Exceptionalism: Class Consciousness and the American Labor Movement," Nick Salvatore, "Response," and Michael Hanagan, "Response," *International Labor and Working-Class History* 26 (Fall 1984): 1–36. See also Sean Wilentz, "Wilentz Answers His Critics," *International Labor and Working-Class History* 28 (Fall 1985): 46–55; and Larry G. Gerber, "Shifting Perspectives on American Exceptionalism: Recent Literature on American Labor Relations and Labor Politics," *Journal of American Studies* 31, no. 2 (August 1997): 253–274.

Chapter 1: Artisans in the New Republic, 1787–1825

In this chapter, I look at the structural and ideological changes that accompanied the transformation of the artisan system of production during the thirty years that followed the ratification of the Constitution. As a manufacturing economy progressed, an older system of workplace relations based on mutuality gave way. Employers and workers increasingly encountered one another as capital and labor, the central issue becoming the "labor question," which Peter Kolchin has astutely defined as "Who should work for whom, under what terms should work be performed, and how should it be compelled or rewarded?" See Peter Kolchin, "The Big Picture: A Comment on David Brion Davis's 'Looking at Slavery from Broader Perspectives,'" *American Historical Review* 105 (April 2000): 467–471. As capitalist marketplace relations evolved, workers organized collectively to protect their livelihoods and place in society, which gave rise to the formation of a labor movement.

The artisan as a feature of the American economic landscape predates the American Revolution. Among the leading works on the artisan in colonial and early America, see especially Billy G. Smith, *The "Lower Sort": Philadelphia's Laboring People, 1750–1800* (Ithaca, NY: Cornell University Press, 1990); Smith, "The Material Lives of Laboring Philadelphians, 1750 to 1800,"

William and Mary Quarterly 38, no. 2 (April 1981): 163–202; Richard Walsh, *Charleston's Sons of Liberty: A Study of Artisans, 1763–1789* (Columbia: University of South Carolina Press, 1959); Henry P. Rosemont, "Benjamin Franklin and the Philadelphia Typographical Strikers of 1786," *Labor History* 22, no. 3 (Summer 1981): 398–429; Simon Middlekauf, *From Privileges to Rights: Work and Politics in Colonial New York City* (Philadelphia: University Pennsylvania Press, 2006); and Thomas M. Doeflinger, *A Vigorous Spirit of Enterprise: Merchants and Economic Development in Revolutionary Philadelphia* (Chapel Hill: University of North Carolina Press, 1986).

The literature on the artisan system of production in the early republic is vast. Among the works that best introduce the key themes are Sean Wilentz, "Artisan Origins of the American Working Class," *International Labor and Working-Class History* 19 (Spring 1981): 1–22; David Brody, "Time and Work during Early American Industrialism," chap. 1 in *In Labor's Cause: Main Themes on the History of the American Worker* (New York: Oxford University Press, 1993); W. J. Rorabaugh, *The Craft Apprentice: From Franklin to the Machine Age in America* (New York: Oxford University Press, 1986); David Montgomery, "The Working Classes of the Pre-Industrial American City, 1780–1830," *Labor History* 9, no. 1 (Winter 1968): 3–22; and William Mulligan, "From Artisan to Proletarian: The Family and the Vocational Education of the Shoemaker in the Handicraft Era," in *Life and Labor: Dimensions of American Working-Class History*, ed. Charles Stephenson and Robert Asher (Albany: State University of New York Press, 1986), 22–36.

Historians have produced a vast literature on the political and social convictions of artisans in the decades surrounding the American Revolution. In particular, they have considered artisans and the ideological tradition of republicanism. Of special interest in understanding this issue are Daniel Vickers, "Competency and Competition: Economic Culture in Early America," *William and*

Mary Quarterly 47, no. 1 (January 1990): 3–29; Rowland Berthoff, "Independence and Attachment, Virtue and Interest: From Republican Citizen to Free Enterpriser, 1787–1837," in *Uprooted Americans: Essays to Honor Oscar Handlin*, ed. Richard Bushman, Kenneth A. Lockridge, and Philip J. Greven (Boston: Little, Brown, 1979), 97–124; Alfred F. Young, "Revolutionary Mechanics," in *Working for Democracy: American Workers from the Revolution to the Present*, ed. Paul Buhle and Alan Dawley (Urbana: University of Illinois Press, 1985), 1–9; Young, "The Mechanics and Jeffersonians: New York, 1789–1801," *Labor History* 5, no. 3 (1964): 247–276; Young, *The Democratic Republicans of New York: The Origins, 1763–1797* (Chapel Hill: University of North Carolina Press, 1967); Young, *Liberty Tree: Ordinary People and the American Revolution* (New York: New York University Press, 2006); Gary Nash, *The Urban Crucible: Social Change, Political Consciousness, and the Origins of the American Revolution* (Cambridge, MA: Harvard University Press, 1979); Donna J. Rilling, "Small Producer Capitalism in Early National Philadelphia," in *The Economy of Early America: Historical Perspectives and New Directions*, ed. Cathy Matson (University Park: Pennsylvania State University Press, 2006); Staughton Lynd, "The Mechanics in New York City Politics, 1774–1788," *Labor History* 5, no. 3 (1964): 215–246; Eric Foner, *Tom Paine and Revolutionary America* (New York: Oxford University Press, 1976); Robert E. Shalhope, "Republicanism and Early American Historiography," *William and Mary Quarterly* 39, no. 2 (April 1982): 334–356; Daniel T. Rodgers, "Republicanism: The Career of a Concept," *Journal of American History* 79, no. 1 (June 1992): 11–38; Drew McCoy, *The Elusive Republic: Political Economy in Jeffersonian America* (Chapel Hill: University of North Carolina Press, 1980); Ronald Schultz, "The Small-Producer Tradition and the Moral Origins of Artisan Radicalism in Philadelphia, 1720–1810," *Past and Present* 127 (May 1990): 84–116; Gary Kornblith, "The Artisanal Response to Capitalist

Transformation," *Journal of the Early Republic* 10, no. 3 (Autumn 1990): 315–321; Kornblith, ed., *The Industrial Revolution in America* (Boston: Houghton Mifflin, 1998); Steven J. Ross, "The Transformation of Republican Ideology," *Journal of the Early Republic* 10, no. 3 (Autumn 1990): 323–330; Carol Lassiter, "Gender, Ideology, and Class in the Early Republic," *Journal of the Early Republic* 10, no. 3 (Autumn 1990): 331–337; and Andrew Shankman, *Crucible of American Democracy: The Struggle to Fuse Egalitarianism and Capitalism in Jeffersonian Pennsylvania* (Lawrence: University Press of Kansas, 2004). The place of manufacturing in the American economy was much disputed in the early republic. To help understand how early Americans framed this debate see especially Lawrence A. Peskin, *Manufacturing Revolution: The Intellectual Origins of Early American Industry* (Baltimore: Johns Hopkins University Press, 2004); "Special Issue on Capitalism in the Early Republic," *Journal of the Early Republic* 16, no. 2 (Summer 1996): 159–308; Michael Brewster Folsom and Steven D. Lubar, *The Philosophy of Manufactures: Early Debates over Industrialization in the United States* (Cambridge, MA: MIT Press, 1982); Cathy D. Matson and Peter S. Onuf, *A Union of Interests: Political and Economic Thought in Revolutionary America* (Lawrence: University Press of Kansas, 1990); Stephen B. Hodin, "The Mechanisms of Monticello: Saving Labor in Jefferson's America," *Journal of the Early Republic* 26, no. 3 (Fall 2006): 377–418; Joyce Appleby, *Capitalism and a New Social Order* (New York: New York University Press, 1976); John C. Van Horne, "The Federal Procession of 1788," talk delivered to the Quarterly Meeting of The Carpenters' Company, July 20, 1987, http://www.ushistory.org/carpentershall/history/procession.htm; Jacob E. Cooke, *Tench Coxe and the Early Republic* (Chapel Hill: University of North Carolina Press, 1978); Frederick B. Tolles, *George Logan of Philadelphia* (New York: Oxford University Press, 1953); Richard J. Twomey, *Jacobins and Jeffersonians:*

Anglo-American Radicalism in the United States, 1790–1820 (New York: Garland, 1989); and Seth Rockman, "The Unfree Origins of American Capitalism," in *The Economy of Early America: Historical Perspectives and New Directions*, ed. Cathy Matson (University Park: Pennsylvania State University Press, 2006), 335–361. Other valuable studies include John R. Nelson, Jr., *Liberty and Property: Political Economy and Policy Making in the New Nation* (Baltimore: Johns Hopkins University Press, 1987); Nelson, "Alexander Hamilton and American Manufacturing: A Reexamination," *Journal of American History* 65, no. 4 (March 1979): 971–995; Tony A. Freyer, *Producers versus Capitalists: Constitutional Conflict in Antebellum America* (Charlottesville: University Press of Virginia, 1994); John E. Sawyer, "The Social Basis of the American System of Manufacturing," *Journal of Economic History* 14, no. 4 (1954): 361–379; Andrew Shankman, "'A New Thing on Earth': Alexander Hamilton, Pro-Manufacturing Republicans, and the Democratization of American Political Economy," *Journal of the Early Republic* 23, no. 3 (Fall 2003): 323–352; Samuel Rezneck, "The Rise and Early Development of Industrial Consciousness in the United States, 1760–1830," *Journal of Economic and Business History* 4 (August 1932): 784–811; and Robert B. Morris, *Government and Labor in Early America* (New York: Harper & Row, 1946).

Much of the debate over political economy focused on the development of American manufactures. Useful analyses of the value of mechanized versus agrarian production in the early republic can be found in John F. Kasson, *Civilizing the Machine: Technology and Republican Values in America, 1776–1900* (New York: Penguin Books, 1976); Leo Marx, *The Machine in the Garden: Technology and the Pastoral Ideal in America* (New York: Oxford University Press, 1964); Carroll Purcell, *The Machine in America: A Social History of Technology* (Baltimore: Johns Hopkins University Press, 1995); Ruth Schwartz Cowan, *A Social History of American Technology* (New York: Oxford

University Press, 1997); Brooke Hindle and Steven Lubar, *Engines of Change: The American Industrial Revolution, 1790–1860* (Washington, DC: Smithsonian Institution Press, 1986); and David Hounshell, *From the American System to Mass Production, 1800–1932: The Development of Manufacturing Technology in the United States* (Baltimore: Johns Hopkins University Press, 1985).

Seaport cities were the primary location for the early rise of manufactures in the New Republic. For Philadelphia, see Cynthia J. Shelton, *The Mills of Manayunk: Industrialization and Social Conflict in the Philadelphia Region, 1787–1837* (Baltimore: Johns Hopkins University Press, 1986); Smith, *The "Lower Sort"*; Diane Lindstrom, *Economic Development in the Philadelphia Region, 1810–1850* (New York: Columbia University Press, 1978); Philip Scranton, *Proprietary Capitalism: The Textile Manufacture at Philadelphia, 1800–1885* (Philadelphia: Temple University Press, 1983); Charles S. Olton, *Artisans for Independence: Philadelphia Mechanics and the American Revolution* (Syracuse, NY: Syracuse University Press, 1975); Sharon V. Salinger, "Artisans, Journeymen, and the Transformation of Labor in Late Eighteenth-Century Philadelphia," *William and Mary Quarterly* 40, no. 1 (January 1983): 62–84; Salinger, *"To Serve Well and Faithfully": Labor and Indentured Servants in Pennsylvania, 1682–1800* (New York: Cambridge University Press, 1987); Ronald Schultz, *The Republic of Labor: Philadelphia Artisans and the Politics of Class, 1720–1830* (New York: Oxford University Press, 1993); Donna J. Rilling, *Making Houses, Crafting Capitalism: Builders in Philadelphia, 1790–1850* (Philadelphia: University of Pennsylvania Press, 2001). On New York, see Sean Wilentz, *Chants Democratic: New York City and the Rise of the American Working Class, 1788–1850* (New York: Oxford University Press, 1984), and Howard B. Rock, *Artisans of the New Republic: The Tradesmen of New York City in the Age of Jefferson* (New York: New York University Press, 1979).

On Baltimore, see Charles G. Steffen, *The Mechanics of Baltimore: Workers and Politics in the Age of Revolution, 1763–1812* (Urbana: University of Illinois Press, 1984); Steffen, "Changes in the Organization of Artisan Production in Baltimore, 1790–1820," *William and Mary Quarterly* 36, no. 1 (January 1979) 101–117; and Rockman, *Scraping By.* Other cities are discussed in Steven J. Ross, *Workers on the Edge: Work, Leisure, and Politics in Industrializing Cincinnati, 1788–1890* (New York: Columbia University Press, 1985), and Susan E. Hirsch, *Roots of the American Working Class: The Industrialization of Crafts in Newark, 1800–1860* (Philadelphia: University of Pennsylvania Press, 1978).

The development of manufacturing in America is usually associated with the transformation of artisan crafts and the rise of factory production in the cities. As a result, changes in rural manufacturing, especially the growing involvement of women in outwork, are frequently minimized in these accounts. Rural manufacturers and outwork are examined in Thomas Dublin, *Transforming Women's Work: New England Lives in the Industrial Revolution* (Ithaca, NY: Cornell University Press, 1994); Dublin, "Women and Outwork in a Nineteenth-Century New England Town, Fitzwilliam, New Hampshire, 1830–1850," in *The Countryside in the Age of Capitalist Transformation: Essays in the Social History of Rural America*, ed. Steven Hahn and Jonathan Prude (Chapel Hill: University of North Carolina Press, 1985), 51–70; Dublin, "Rural Putting-Out Work in Early Nineteenth-Century New England: Women and the Transition to Capitalism in the Countryside," *New England Quarterly* 64, no. 4 (December 1991): 531–573; Mary H. Blewett, "Women Shoeworkers and Domestic Ideology: Rural Outwork in Early Nineteenth-Century Essex County," *New England Quarterly* 60, no. 3 (September 1987) 403–428; Blewett, *Men, Women, and Work: Class, Gender, and Protest in the New England Shoe Industry, 1780–1910* (Urbana: University of Illinois Press, 1988); Paul G. Faler,

Mechanics and Manufacturers in the Early Industrial Revolution: Lynn, Massachusetts, 1780–1860 (Albany: State University of New York Press, 1981); Marla R. Miller, "Gender, Artisanry, and Craft Tradition in Early New England: The View through the Eye of a Needle," *William and Mary Quarterly* 60, no. 4 (October 2003): 743–776; Laurel Thatcher Ulrich, *The Age of Homespun: Objects and Stories in the Creation of an American Myth* (New York: Alfred A. Knopf, 2001); Rolla M. Tryon, *Household Manufactures in the United States, 1640–1860* (Chicago: University of Chicago Press, 1917); Christopher Clark, *The Roots of Rural Capitalism: Western Massachusetts, 1780–1860* (Ithaca, NY: Cornell University Press, 1990); Jeanne Boydston, *Home and Work: Housework, Wages, and the Ideology of Labor in the Early Republic* (New York: Oxford University Press, 1990); Groneman and Norton, *"To Toil the Livelong Day"*; and Christine Stansell, *City of Women: Sex and Class in New York, 1789–1860* (New York: Alfred A. Knopf, 1986).

Beginning in the 1780s, both employing masters and wage-earning journeymen developed distinct and increasingly opposed interests. When the journeymen formed associations among themselves and engaged in "turnouts" in defense of their economic and social well-being, employers challenged the workers' unions in court as illegal conspiracies in restraint of trade. These legal battles have been ably probed in Christopher L. Tomlins, *Law, Labor, and Ideology in the Early American Republic* (New York: Cambridge University Press, 1993); Tomlins, "Criminal Conspiracy and Early Labor Combinations: Massachusetts, 1824–1840," *Labor History* 28, no. 3 (Summer 1987): 370–386; and Christopher L. Tomlins and Andrew J. King, eds., *Labor Law in America: Historical and Critical Essays* (Baltimore: Johns Hopkins University Press, 1992), especially the essays in Tomlins and King by Robert J. Steinfeld, "The *Philadelphia Cordwainers'* Case of 1806: The Struggle over Alternative Legal Constructions of a Free Market in Labor," 20–43, and Victoria C. Hattam,

"Courts and Questions of Class: Judicial Regulation of Labor under the Common Law Doctrine of Criminal Conspiracy," 44–70. These issues are also discussed in Morton J. Horwitz, *The Transformation of American Law, 1780–1860* (Cambridge, MA: Harvard University Press, 1979); Walter Nelles, "The First American Labor Case," *Yale Law Journal* 41, no. 2 (December 1931): 165–200; Sean Wilentz, "Conspiracy, Power, and the Early Labor Movement: The People v. James Melvin et al., 1811," *Labor History* 24, no. 4 (Fall 1984): 572–579; Wythe Holt, "Labour Conspiracy Cases in the United States, 1805–1842: Bias and Legitimation in Common Law Adjudication," *Osgoode Hall Law Journal* 22, no. 4 (Winter 1984): 591–663; Edwin E. Witte, "Early American Labor Cases," *Yale Law Journal* 35, no. 7 (May 1926): 825–837; Marjorie S. Turner, *The Early American Labor Conspiracy Cases: Their Place in Labor Law, A Reinterpretation* (San Diego, CA: San Diego State College Press, 1967); Raymond L. Hogler, "Law, Ideology, and Industrial Discipline: The Conspiracy Doctrine and the Rise of the Factory System," *Dickinson Law Review* 91, no. 3 (Spring 1987): 697–745; Albert S. Konefsky, "'As Best to Subserve Their Own Interests': Lemuel Shaw, Labor Conspiracy, and Fellow Servants," *Law and History Review* 7, no. 1 (Spring 1989): 219–239; Ian M. G. Quimby, "The Cordwainers Protest: A Crisis in Labor Relations," *Winterthur Portfolio* 3 (1967): 83–101; and Brian Greenberg, "Class Conflict and the Demise of the Artisan Order: The Cordwainers' 1805 Strike and 1806 Conspiracy Trial," *Pennsylvania Legacies* 14, no. 1 (Spring 2014): 6–11.

The speechmakers and participants in the parades and events that accompanied the official opening of the Erie Canal in 1825 celebrated the completion of the waterway as a symbol of the benefits that flowed from harmony and united effort. In this they failed to acknowledge the growing divide between employers and workers. On the Erie Canal, see Peter Way, *Common Labor: Workers and the Digging of North American Canals, 1780–1860*

(Baltimore: Johns Hopkins University Press, 1993); Carol Sheriff, *The Artificial River: The Erie Canal and the Paradox of Progress, 1817–1862* (New York: Hill & Wang, 1996); Peter L. Bernstein, *Wedding of the Waters: The Erie Canal and the Making of a Great Nation* (New York: W. W. Norton, 2005); and Paul E. Johnson, *A Shopkeeper's Millennium: Society and Revivals in Rochester, New York, 1815–1837* (New York: Hill & Wang, 1978).

Chapter 2: Labor in the Age of Jackson, 1825–1843

A revolution in the transportation of goods and people during the first half of the nineteenth century opened new markets and encouraged the growth of manufactures in the United States. According to the historian Sean Wilentz, in cities across the United States, a pattern of "metropolitan industrialization" developed, characterized by an ever-growing number of larger, machineless, manufacturing establishments employing at least twenty workers and turning out an impressive quantity of consumer goods. Although earlier artisan shop production persisted, for most journeymen work became more specialized and wage labor a lifelong pursuit. See especially Wilentz, *Chants Democratic*, in which he focuses on New York City. For the geography of industrialism in these years, see Charles Sellers, *The Market Revolution: Jacksonian America, 1815–1846* (New York: Oxford University Press, 1991); John Lauritz Larson, *The Market Revolution in America: Liberty, Ambition, and the Eclipse of the Common Good* (New York: Cambridge University Press, 2010); David A. Zonderman, *Aspirations and Anxieties: New England Workers and the Mechanized Factory System, 1815–1850* (New York: Oxford University Press, 1992); James L. Huston, *Securing the Fruits of Labor: The American Concept of Wealth Distribution, 1765–1900* (Baton Rouge: Louisiana State University Press, 1998); Jonathan Prude, *The Coming of Industrial Order: Town and Factory Life in Rural Massachusetts, 1810–1860* (New York:

Cambridge University Press, 1983); Vera Shlakman, *Economic History of a Factory Town: A Study of Chicopee, Massachusetts* (New York: Octagon Books, 1969); Faler, *Mechanics and Manufacturers in the Early Industrial Revolution; Thomas Dublin, Women at Work: The Transformation of Work and Community in Lowell, Massachusetts, 1826–1860* (New York: Columbia University Press, 1979); and William A. Sullivan, *The Industrial Worker in Pennsylvania, 1800–1840* (Harrisburg: Pennsylvania Historical and Museum Commission, 1955).

The characterization of workers' response to economic and social changes as reflected by certain ideal types is drawn from Alan Dawley and Paul Faler, "Working-Class Culture and Politics in the Industrial Revolution: Sources of Loyalism and Rebellion," *Journal of Social History* 9 (Summer 1976): 466–480; Paul Faler, "Cultural Aspects of the Industrial Revolution; Lynn, Massachusetts Shoemakers and Industrial Morality, 1826–1860," *Labor History* 15, no. 3 (Summer 1974): 367–394; Bruce Laurie, *Working People of Philadelphia, 1800–1850* (Philadelphia: Temple University Press, 1980); and Laurie, "'Nothing on Compulsion': Life Styles of Philadelphia Artisans, 1820–1860," *Labor History* 15, no. 3 (Summer 1974): 337–366. For examples of the persistence of traditional patterns, see Herbert G. Gutman, "Work, Culture, and Society in Industrializing America, 1815–1919," chap. 1 in *Work, Culture, and Society in Industrializing America*; Prude, *The Coming of Industrial Order*; Prude, "Social Conflict in the Early Mills," in *The Industrial Revolution in America*, ed. Gary J. Kornblith (Boston: Houghton Mifflin, 1998), 40–53; Barbara M. Tucker, *Samuel Slater and the Origins of the American Textile Industry, 1790–1860* (Ithaca, NY: Cornell University Press, 1984); W. J. Rorabaugh, *The Alcoholic Republic: An American Tradition* (New York: Oxford University Press, 1979); Caroline F. Ware, *The Early New England Cotton Manufacture: A Study in Industrial Beginnings* (New York: Russell & Russell, 1966); Mulligan, "From Artisan to Proletarian"; and

William Sisson, "From Farm to Factory: Work Values and Discipline in Two Early Textile Mills," *Working Papers from the Regional Economic Research* 4 (1981): 1–27.

Analysis of the Second Great Awakening, which unfolded during the 1820s and 1830s, as a factor in the lives of workers is found in the books of Paul Johnson (on Rochester), Bruce Laurie (on Philadelphia), and Paul Faler (on Lynn) cited earlier. Other works in which it is discussed include Jama Lazerow, *Religion and the Working Class in Antebellum America* (Washington, DC: Smithsonian Institution Press, 1995); Lazerow, "Religion and Labor Reform in Antebellum America: The World of William Field Young," *American Quarterly* 38, no. 2 (Summer 1986): 265–286; Whitney R. Cross, *The Burned-Over District: The Social and Intellectual History of Enthusiastic Religion in Western New York, 1800–1850* (Ithaca, NY: Cornell University Press, 1950); Nancy A. Hewitt, *Women's Activism and Social Change: Rochester, New York, 1822–1872* (Ithaca, NY: Cornell University Press, 1984); and William R. Sutton, *Journeymen for Jesus: Evangelical Artisans Confront Capitalism in Jacksonian Baltimore* (University Park: Pennsylvania State University Press, 1998). See also David Montgomery, "The Shuttle and the Cross: Weavers and Artisans in the Kensington Riots of 1844," *Journal of Social History* 5, no. 4 (Summer 1972): 411–446; Michael Feldberg, *The Philadelphia Riots of 1944: A Study of Ethnic Conflict* (Westport, CT: Greenwood Press, 1975); and Ian Tyrrell, *Sobering Up: From Temperance to Prohibition in Antebellum America* (Westport, CT: Greenwood Press, 1979).

The issues that concerned radical workingmen's and workingwomen's movements in Lowell and Lynn, Massachusetts, in these years has been described with great subtlety in works by Thomas Dublin (*Women at Work*) and Paul G. Faler (*Mechanics and Manufacturers*). See also Thomas Dublin, "Women, Work, and Protest in the Early Lowell Mills: 'The Oppressing Hand of

Avarice Would Enslave Us,'" *Labor History* 16, no. 1 (Winter 1975): 99–116; Harriet H. Robinson, *Loom and Spindle; or, Life among the Early Mill Girls* (Kailua, HI: Press Pacifica, 1976); Edward Pessen, *Most Uncommon Jacksonians: The Radical Leaders of the Early Labor Movement* (Albany: State University of New York Press, 1967); Pessen, *Jacksonian America: Society, Personality, and Politics* (Homewood, IL: Dorsey Press, 1969); Pessen, "The Working Men's Party Revisited," *Labor History* 4, no. 3 (Fall 1963): 203–226; Walter Hugins, *Jacksonian Democracy and the Working Class: A Study of the New York Workingmen's Movement, 1829–1837* (Stanford, CA: Stanford University Press, 1960); Ronald Schultz, "God and Workingmen: Popular Religion and the Formation of Philadelphia's Working Class, 1790–1830," in *Religion in a Revolutionary Age*, ed. Ronald Hoffman and Peter J. Albert (Charlottesville: University Press of Virginia, 1994), 125–155; Blewett, *Men, Women, and Work;* Theresa A. Murphy, *Ten Hours' Labor: Religion, Reform, and Gender in Early New England* (Ithaca, NY: Cornell University Press, 1992); Benita Eisler, ed., *The Lowell Offering: Writings by New England Mill Women (1840–1845)* (Philadelphia: J. B. Lippincott, 1977); Thomas Dublin, ed., *Farm to Factory: Women's Letters, 1830–1860*, 2nd ed. (New York: Columbia University Press, 1993); Nancy Zaroulis, "Daughters of Freemen: The Female Operatives and the Beginnings of the Labor Movement," in *Cotton Was King: A History of Lowell, Massachusetts*, ed. Arthur L. Eno (Lowell, MA: Lowell Historical Society, 1976), 105–126; David R. Roediger and Philip S. Foner, *Our Own Time: A History of American Labor and the Working Day* (Westport, CT: Greenwood Press, 1989); Stansell, *City of Women;* Louis H. Arky, "The Mechanics' Union of Trade Associations and the Formation of the Philadelphia Workingmen's Movement," *Pennsylvania Magazine of History and Biography* 76, no. 2 (April 1952): 142–176; and Thomas Bender, *Toward an Urban Vision: Ideas and Institutions in*

Nineteenth-Century America (Lexington: University Press of Kentucky, 1975).

During the 1820s through the 1840s, politics in America underwent significant change. Among the leading studies of the new politics of the Jacksonian era are Richard P. McCormick, *The Second American Party System: Party Formation in the Jacksonian Era* (Chapel Hill: University of North Carolina Press, 1966); Marvin Meyers, *The Jacksonian Persuasion: Politics and Belief* (Stanford, CA: Stanford University Press, 1957); Jean H. Baker, *The Affairs of Party: The Political Culture of Northern Democrats in the Mid-Nineteenth Century* (Ithaca, NY: Cornell University Press, 1983); and Lee Benson, *The Concept of Jacksonian Democracy: New York as a Test Case* (Princeton, NJ: Princeton University Press, 1961). See also Daniel Walker Howe, *The Political Culture of American Whigs* (Chicago: University of Chicago Press, 1979); Howe, *What Hath God Wrought: The Transformation of America, 1815–1848* (New York: Oxford University Press, 2007); and Douglass T. Miller, *Jacksonian Aristocracy: Class and Democracy in New York, 1830–1860* (New York: Oxford University Press, 1967).

Chapter 3: The Industrial Worker in Free Labor America

The rise of new labor history in the 1970s was heralded by the publication of Alan Dawley, *Class and Community: The Industrial Revolution in Lynn* (Cambridge, MA: Harvard University Press, 1976), and Paul Faler's *Mechanics and Manufacturers in the Early Industrial Revolution*. Also on Lynn, see William H. Mulligan, Jr., *The Shoemakers of Lynn, Massachusetts, 1850–1880: The Family during the Transition from Hand to Machine Labor* (Lewiston, NY: Edwin Mellen Press, 2006). Other new labor historians followed in the wake of Faler and Dawley and, like them, focused on the communities that experienced the social, economic, and political changes wrought by the coming of the industrial order in America. Outstanding among these community studies are Laurie, *Working People of Philadelphia, 1800–1850*; Daniel J. Walkowitz, *Worker City, Company Town: Iron and Cotton-Worker Protest in Troy and Cohoes, New York, 1855–84* (Urbana: University of Illinois Press, 1978); Hirsch, *Roots of the American Working Class*; Wilentz, *Chants Democratic*; Ross, *Workers on the Edge*; John Cumbler, *Working-Class Community in Industrial America: Work, Leisure, and Struggle in Two Industrial Cities, 1800–1930* (Westport, CT: Greenwood Press, 1979); and Brian Greenberg, *Worker and Community: Response to Industrialization in a Nineteenth-Century American City, Albany, New York, 1850–1884* (Albany: State University of New York Press, 1985).

The ideas and social values of the broad-based movement for reform of American society that arose in the 1840s can be found in John F. C. Harrison, *Quest for the New Moral World: Robert Owen and the Owenites in Britain and America* (New York: Scribner's, 1969); Carl J. Guarneri, *The Utopian Alternative: Fourierism in Nineteenth-Century America* (Ithaca, NY: Cornell University Press, 1991); Arthur E. Bestor, *Backwoods Utopias: The Sectarian and Owenite Phases of Communitarian Socialism in America, 1663–1829* (Philadelphia: University of Pennsylvania Press, 1950); and John Ashworth, *"Agrarians" and "Aristocrats": Party Political Ideology in the United States, 1837–1846* (New York: Cambridge University Press, 1987). Massachusetts was often at the center of labor reform in the 1840s. See especially David A. Zonderman, *Uneasy Allies: Working for Labor Reform in Nineteenth-Century Boston* (Amherst: University of Massachusetts Press, 2011); Brian Greenberg, "Volatile Alliances: Middle-Class Reformers and Working-Class Activists in Nineteenth-Century Boston," *Reviews in American History* 41, no. 2 (June 2013): 271–276; Mary H. Blewett, *Constant Turmoil: The Politics of Industrial Life in Nineteenth-Century New England*

(Amherst: University of Massachusetts Press, 2000); and Dublin, *Women at Work*. Works that focus on specific labor reforms in these years are Jonathan Grossman, "Co-operative Foundries," *New York History* 24, no. 2 (April 1943): 196–210, and Roediger and Foner, *Our Own Time*.

A number of excellent books offer insight into the immigrant experience in America in the 1840s and 1850s. Included among these are John Bodnar, ed., *The Ethnic Experience in Pennsylvania* (Lewisburg, PA: Bucknell University Press, 1973); Victor R. Greene, *The Slavic Community on Strike: Immigrant Labor in Pennsylvania Anthracite* (Notre Dame, IN: University of Notre Dame Press, 1968); Oscar Handlin, *The Uprooted: The Epic Story of the Great Migrations that Made the American People* (Boston: Little, Brown, 1951); Handlin, *Boston's Immigrants: A Study in Acculturation* (Cambridge, MA: Harvard University Press, 1959); Bruce Laurie, Theodore Hershberg, and George Alter, "Immigrants and Social History: The Philadelphia Experience, 1850–1880," *Journal of Social History* 9, no. 2 (Winter 1975): 219–248; Howard M. Gitelman, "The Waltham System and the Coming of the Irish," *Labor History* 8, no. 3 (Fall 1967): 227–253; Clifton K. Yearly, Jr., *Britons in American Labor* (Baltimore: Johns Hopkins University Press, 1957); Kathleen Neils Conzen, *Immigrant Milwaukee, 1836–1860: Acculturation and Community in a Frontier City* (Cambridge, MA: Harvard University Press, 1976); Harmut Keil and John B. Jentz, eds., *German Workers in Industrial Chicago, 1850–1910: A Comparative Perspective* (DeKalb: Northern Illinois University Press, 1983); Charlotte Erickson, ed., *Invisible Immigrants: The Adaptation of English and Scottish Immigrants in Nineteenth-Century America* (Ithaca, NY: Cornell University Press, 1990); and Douglas V. Shaw, *The Making of an Immigrant City: Ethnic and Cultural Conflict in Jersey City, New Jersey, 1850–1877* (New York: Arno Press, 1976).

On the rise of nativism in these years, see John Higham, *Strangers in the Land: Patterns of American Nativism, 1860–1925*

(New Brunswick, NJ: Rutgers University Press, 1955); Ray Allen Billington, *The Protestant Crusade, 1800–1860: A Study of the Origins of American Nativism* (New York: Macmillan, 1938); Montgomery, "The Shuttle and the Cross"; Bruce Laurie, "Fire Companies and Gangs in Southwark: The 1840s," in *The Peoples of Philadelphia: A History of Ethnic Group and Lower-Class Life, 1790–1940*, ed. Allen F. Davis and Mark H. Haller (Philadelphia: University of Pennsylvania Press, 1973), 71–87.

Much about the African American work experience outside of plantation slavery can be found in the autobiographical works of Frederick Douglass as well as in biographies of him. See especially Douglass, *Narrative of the Life of Frederick Douglass*, and William S. McFeely, *Frederick Douglass* (New York: W. W. Norton, 1991). See also Julius Jacobson, ed., *The Negro and the American Labor Movement* (New York: Doubleday, 1968). Since the publication of David Roediger's *The Wages of Whiteness: Race and the Making of the American Working Class* (New York: Verso, 1991) whiteness studies – how diverse groups, particularly immigrant white workers, came to identify themselves, and to be identified by others, as "white" – has dominated our understanding of the history of racism in America.

The prevailing paradigm among older labor historians on the rise of the labor movement in the 1850s and 1860s was expressed by Norman Ware, *The Industrial Worker, 1840–1860*. My critique of Ware's use of the "binary model" employs the insights into the antebellum labor movement found in Sean Wilentz, "The Rise of the American Working Class, 1776–1877: A Survey." A key figure in the labor movement in the 1850s was William Sylvis, a founder of the the Iron Molder's International Union and the National Labor Union. On Sylvis, see James C. Sylvis, *The Life, Speeches, Labors, and Essays of William H. Sylvis* (New York: Augustus M. Kelley, 1968); Jonathan P. Grossman, *William Sylvis, Pioneer of American Labor: A Study of the Labor Movement during the Era of the Civil War* (New York: Columbia University Press, 1945);

James E. Cebula, *The Glory and Despair of Challenge and Change: A History of the Molders Union* (Cincinnati, OH: International Molders and Allied Workers Union, 1976); Henry E. Hoagland, "The Rise of the Iron Molders' International Union: A Study in Trade Unionism," *American Economic Review* 3, no. 2 (June 1913): 296–313; and David Montgomery, "William H. Sylvis and the Search for Working-Class Citizenship," in *Labor Leaders in America*, ed. Melvyn Dubofsky and Warren Van Tine (Urbana: University of Illinois Press, 1987), 3–29.

The legal issue of labor as a conspiracy was again confronted by the courts in the 1850s and 1860s. See especially Leonard W. Levy, *The Law of the Commonwealth and Chief Justice Shaw* (New York: Oxford University Press, 1987), and Robert J. Steinfeld, *The Invention of Free Labor: The Employment Relation in English and American Law and Culture, 1350–1870* (Chapel Hill: University of North Carolina Press, 1991). On the importance of the concept of free labor in these years, see Eric Foner, *Free Soil, Free Labor, Free Men: The Ideology of the Republican Party Before the Civil War* (New York: Oxford University Press, 1970); Greenberg, *Worker and Community*; Jonathan A. Glickstein, *Concepts of Free Labor in Antebellum America* (New Haven, CT: Yale University Press 1991); and Sven Beckert, *The Monied Metropolis: New York City and the Consolidation of the American Bourgeoisie, 1850–1896* (New York: Cambridge University Press, 1993).

Chapter 4: From the Civil War to the Panic of 1873

Since the late 1960s the leading interpretation of the impact of the Civil War and Reconstruction on the labor movement has been David Montgomery, *Beyond Equality: Labor and the Radical Republicans, 1862–1872* (New York: Alfred A. Knopf, 1967). Also of importance to our making sense of workers' response to the Civil War are Iver Bernstein, *The New York City Draft Riots: Their Significance for American Society and Politics in the Age of the Civil War* (New York: Oxford University Press, 1990), and Mark A. Lause, *Free Labor: The Civil War and the Making of an American Working Class* (Urbana: University of Illinois Press, 2015).

Many of the histories of labor in the nineteenth century already cited are especially useful in understanding the changes in work and labor during the Civil War and in the decade following it. Of particular note are Commons et al., *History of Labour in the United States*, vol. 2; Rayback, *A History of American Labor*; Dubofsky, *Industrialism and the American Worker*; Dulles and Dubofsky, *Labor in America*; Foner, *History of the Labor Movement in the United States*; and Laurie, *Artisans into Workers*. See also Ware, *The Labor Movement in the United States, 1860–1895*; Chester McArthur Destler, *American Radicalism, 1865–1901* (Chicago: Quadrangle Books, 1946); Irwin Yellowitz, *The Position of the Worker in American Society, 1865–1896* (Englewood Cliffs, NJ: Prentice Hall, 1969); Gerald N. Grob, *Workers and Utopia: A Study of Ideological Conflict in the American Labor Movement, 1865–1900* (Chicago: Quadrangle Books, 1969); and Brian Greenberg, "Cameron, Andrew Carr," "Coxe, Tench," and "Sylvis, William H.," in American National Biography Online, http://www.anb.org/articles.

The Great Lockout is discussed in Walkowitz, *Worker City, Company Town*, and in Greenberg, *Worker and Community*. On the role played by William Sylvis, see Sylvis, *The Life, Speeches, Labors, and Essays of William H. Sylvis*; Grossman, *William Sylvis, Pioneer of American Labor*; Grossman, "Co-operative Foundries"; Greenberg, "Sylvis"; Cebula, *The Glory and Despair of Challenge and Change*; Hoagland, "The Rise of the Iron Molders' International Union"; and Montgomery, "William H. Sylvis and the Search for Working-Class Citizenship."

Works that examine the economic perspective shared by large-scale manufacturers include Beckert, *The Monied Metropolis*; Robert P. Sharkey, *Money, Class, and Party: An*

Economic Study of the Civil War and Reconstruction (Baltimore: Johns Hopkins University Press, 1959); Edward C. Kirkland, *Dream and Thought in the Business Community* (Ithaca, NY: Cornell University Press, 1956); and Kirkland, *Industry Comes of Age: Business, Labor and Public Policy, 1860–1897* (New York: Holt, Rinehart & Winston, 1961).

Of particular note on labor reform in Massachusetts is Zonderman, *Uneasy Allies*. Important earlier studies of the postwar eight-hours movement include Roediger and Foner, *Our Own Time*; Timothy Messer-Kruse, "Eight Hours, Greenbacks, and 'Chinamen': Wendell Phillips, Ira Steward, and the Fate of Labor Reform in Massachusetts," *Labor History* 42, no. 2 (2001): 133–158; Irwin Yellowitz, "Eight Hours and the Bricklayers' Strike of 1868 in New York City," in *Essays in the History of New York City: A Memorial to Sidney Pomerantz*, ed. Irwin Yellowitz (Port Washington, NY: Kennikat Press, 1978), 78–100; and Brian Greenberg, "Wendell Phillips and the Idea of Industrial Democracy in Early Postbellum America," in *The Struggle for Equality: Essays on Sectional Conflict, the Civil War, and the Long Reconstruction*, ed. Orville Vernon Burton, Jerald Podair, and Jennifer L. Weber (Charlottesville: University of Virginia Press, 2011), 137–152.

On Kate Mullany, see Carole Turbin, *Working Women of Collar City: Gender, Class, and Community in Troy, New York, 1864–86* (Urbana: University of Illinois Press, 1992), and National Park Service, Kate Mullany National Historic Site, www.kate mullanynhs.org; see also "Kate Mullany: A Trade Union Pioneer," http://www.katemullanynhs.org/node/15.

Epilogue: A Tradition of Labor Protest Persists

As the social relations of production sharpened in the aftermath of the panic of 1873, so too did the workers' struggle to achieve economic democracy in America. Here again David Montgomery's

Beyond Equality is the best starting place. In addition to the general labor histories already noted, see Troy Rondinone, *The Great Industrial War: Framing Class Conflict in the Media, 1865–1950* (New Brunswick, NJ: Rutgers University Press, 2010); Leon Fink, *Workingmen's Democracy: The Knights of Labor and American Politics* (Urbana: University of Illinois Press, 1983); Rosanne Currarino, *The Labor Question in America: Economic Democracy in the Gilded Age* (Urbana: University of Illinois Press, 2011); Kim Voss, *The Making of American Exceptionalism: The Knights of Labor and Class Formation in the Nineteenth Century* (Ithaca, NY: Cornell University Press, 1993); Wayne Broehl, *The Molly Maguires* (Cambridge, MA: Harvard University Press, 1964); Milton Derber, *The American Idea of Industrial Democracy* (Urbana: University of Illinois Press, 1975); and Alexander Saxton, *The Indispensable Enemy: Labor and the Anti-Chinese Movement in California* (Berkeley: University of California Press, 1971).

On Samuel Gompers and other leading labor figures in the 1870s and 1880s, see Ware, *The Labor Movement in the United States, 1860–1895*; Samuel Gompers, *Seventy Years of Life and Labor* (New York: E. P. Dutton, 1925); Stuart Bruce Kaufman, Peter J. Albert, and Grace Palladino, eds., *Samuel Gompers Papers*, 12 vols. (Urbana: University of Illinois Press, 1989–2010); Harold C. Livesay, *Samuel Gompers and Organized Labor in America* (Boston: Addison-Wesley Educational, 1987); Bernard Mandel, *Samuel Gompers: A Biography* (New York: Penguin, 1963); Brian Greenberg, "Samuel Gompers and the American Federation of Labor," in *American Reform and Reformers: A Biographical Dictionary*, ed. Randall M. Miller and Paul A. Cimbala (Westport, CT: Greenwood Press, 1995), 270–286; Terence V. Powderly, *Thirty Years of Labor, 1859–1889* (Columbus, OH: Excelsior Publishing House, 1890); and Craig Phelan, *Grand Master Workman: Terence Powderly and the Knights of Labor* (Westport, CT: Greenwood Press, 2000).

On the significance of Labor Day in the history of the labor movement, see Michael Kazin and Steven J. Ross, "America's Labor Day: The Dilemma of a Workers' Celebration," *Journal of American History* 78, no. 4 (March 1992): 1294–1323; Theodore F. Watts, *The First Labor Day Parade, Tuesday, September 5, 1882: Media Mirrors to Labor's Icons* (Silver Spring, MD: Phoenix Rising, 1983); Jonathan Grossman, "Who Is the Father of Labor Day?" *Labor History* 14, no. 4 (Fall 1973): 612–623; and Ware, *The Labor Movement in the United States, 1860–1895.*

INDEX

Page references to Figures are followed by *f*

The Dawning of American Labor: The New Republic to the Industrial Age,
First Edition. Brian Greenberg.
© 2018 John Wiley & Sons, Inc. Published 2018 by John Wiley & Sons, Inc.